Macro and Microeconomics Through Calculus

Roggie Clark

Continue Learning At Our Website: Roggieclarkbooks.com

Continue exploring educational resources, tools, books, workbooks, and learning materials designed to help readers continue building knowledge and practical skills. Visit: www.roggieclarkbooks.com

Inside you'll find:

- Educational worksheets
- Beginner-friendly guides
- Printable activities
- Companion materials for books and courses

A growing library of educational content for readers, collectors, learners, parents, teachers, and lifelong students.

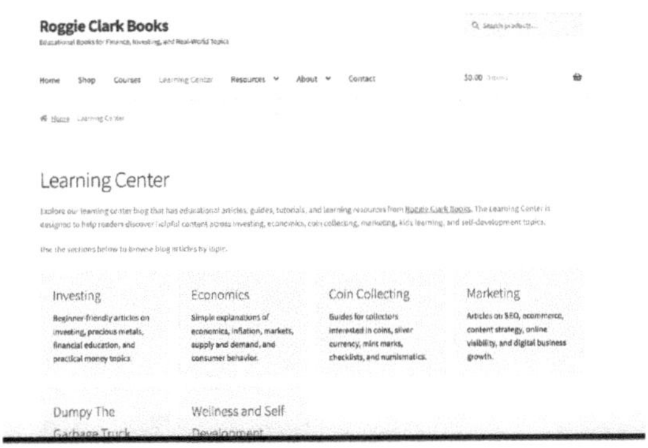

Learn Macro and Micro Economics, With This One Book

Whether you're a student, a professional, or simply someone eager to understand the world around you, this book is your perfect introduction to the fundamentals of micro and macroeconomics.

https://www.amazon.com/Macro-Micro-Economics-Workbook-Beginners-ebook/dp/B0FVPMFX6B

The Strategic Guide to U.S. Mint Gold and Silver Coin Investing

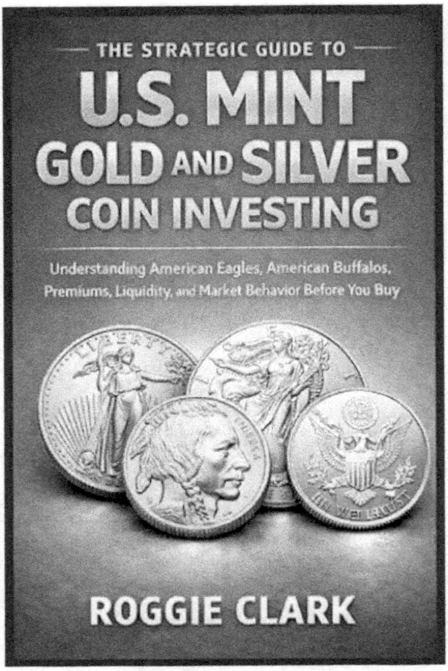

Rather than offering a general introduction to precious metals, this guide examines how American Gold Eagles, American Gold Buffalos, and Silver American Eagles behave in real investor markets.

https://www.amazon.com/Strategic-Guide-U-S-Silver-Investing/dp/B0GQKJF9K6

Copyright

Title: Macro and Microeconomics Through Calculus
Author: Roggie Clark

Cover Design: Roggie Clark
Editing: Renee' Clark

Printed in the United States of America

Disclaimer

The views and opinions expressed in this publication are those of the author and do not necessarily reflect the official policies, positions, opinions, or viewpoints of any individual, company, organization, institution, agency, or entity referenced or mentioned within this work.

The author is not necessarily affiliated with, endorsed by, sponsored by, or compensated by any individuals, companies, organizations, brands, institutions, products, or services referenced within this publication unless specifically stated otherwise. Any examples, sample situations, stories, illustrations, or scenarios presented may be fictionalized or simplified for educational purposes. Any resemblance to actual persons, living or dead, businesses, or events is purely coincidental unless otherwise stated.

The information, ideas, strategies, concepts, techniques, opinions, suggestions, and educational materials contained in this publication are provided on an "as is" basis without warranties of any kind, either express or implied. While every effort has been made to provide accurate and current information, neither the author nor the publisher makes any representations or warranties regarding the completeness, accuracy, reliability, suitability, or applicability of the information presented.

This publication is intended solely for educational and informational purposes and should not be interpreted as professional advice of any kind, including but not limited to financial, investment, legal, tax, business, medical, mental health, educational, psychological, or other professional guidance. Readers should conduct their own independent research and consult appropriately qualified professionals before making decisions that may affect their finances, health, business, education, legal matters, personal circumstances, or other important areas of life.

Results, outcomes, and experiences may vary significantly among individuals. Neither the author nor the publisher guarantees any specific outcomes, results, earnings, performance improvements, personal achievements, or benefits resulting from the use of information contained in this publication.

By reading, accessing, or using this publication, you acknowledge and agree that the author and publisher shall not be held liable for any direct, indirect, incidental, consequential, financial, personal, emotional, or other damages, losses, or claims arising from the use, misuse, interpretation, or application of information contained within this publication. You assume full responsibility for any actions, decisions, and outcomes resulting from the use of this material.

Image Credits and Public Domain Notice

All images, illustrations, graphics, photographs, visual references, and related materials included in this publication are believed to be in the public domain, used under applicable licenses or permissions, created by the author or publisher, or obtained from sources that clearly identify them as available for lawful use.

The author and publisher have made a good faith effort to use only visual materials that are lawfully available for use and distribution. Where applicable, images and visual materials may have been resized, cropped, edited, enhanced, stylized, modified, reformatted, or arranged for educational, informational, design, formatting, or presentation purposes.

This publication is intended for educational, informational, and illustrative purposes only. The inclusion of any image, artwork, photograph, visual reference, symbol, historical material, design, or graphic element is not intended to claim ownership over public domain materials or any third-party intellectual property rights that remain with their respective owners.

If you believe any image or visual material included in this publication has been used in error, please contact the author or publisher so the matter may be reviewed and corrected in future editions or releases if necessary.

Any factual information, specifications, historical references, values, descriptions, statistics, or related content accompanying visual materials are provided for general informational purposes only and may change over time. Readers should conduct their own independent research and consult appropriate sources or qualified professionals when making decisions based on information presented in this publication.

This publication is independently produced and is not affiliated with, endorsed by, sponsored by, or associated with any company, organization, government agency, institution, trademark holder, or third party unless specifically stated otherwise.

Table of Contents

Introduction

Economics is ultimately a study of relationships, decisions, and change. Prices rise and fall, consumers adjust what they purchase, businesses change production as costs and revenues shift, investment accumulates over time, and economic growth can accelerate or slow.

Introductory economic theory allows many of these relationships to be described with words, graphs, and relatively simple equations. More advanced economic analysis, however, often requires us to determine exactly how quickly something is changing, how one variable responds to another, or where an economic decision reaches its optimal point. This is where **calculus** becomes especially valuable. Rather than replacing economic reasoning, calculus provides a mathematical framework for expressing economic relationships more precisely and analyzing how those relationships behave when conditions change.

Throughout this book, calculus will be treated as an analytical tool rather than a collection of procedures to memorize. The purpose is to connect the mathematics directly to the economics so that derivatives, integrals, optimization techniques, and mathematical functions have clear economic meanings. The equations matter because they allow us to answer questions about consumers, firms, markets, production, growth, and decision-making with greater precision.

Why Calculus Matters in Economic Analysis

If you have studied economics before, you have probably encountered the word "marginal" repeatedly. Economists discuss marginal cost, marginal revenue, marginal benefit, marginal utility, marginal product, and many other marginal relationships because economic decisions frequently depend less on the total amount of something and more on what happens when that amount changes.

Consider a business that currently produces 1,000 units of a product. Knowing the company's total production cost is useful, but management may also want to know what happens to cost if production increases. The important question becomes not simply "What does production cost?" but "How does total cost change as production changes?"

Calculus allows us to analyze that question mathematically.

If total cost is represented by:

$$C(q)$$

where q represents quantity produced, then the derivative can be written as:

C'(q)

or:

dC/dq

The derivative measures the rate at which total cost changes with respect to output. Economically, this gives us the **marginal cost function**.

This same mathematical relationship appears throughout economics:

- The derivative of total revenue can give us **marginal revenue**.
- The derivative of total benefit can give us **marginal benefit**.
- The derivative of utility can help us examine marginal utility.
- The derivative of production with respect to an input can help us examine marginal product.
- The derivative of an economic variable with respect to time can help us examine how quickly that variable is growing or declining.

Calculus therefore becomes especially useful whenever an economic problem involves a rate of change.

It becomes even more powerful when the economic problem involves **optimization**. Many economic decisions involve choosing a value that maximizes or minimizes something. A firm may seek to maximize profit, a consumer may seek to maximize utility subject to a budget constraint, or a producer may seek to minimize the cost of achieving a particular level of output.

Suppose a firm's profit is represented by revenue minus cost:

$$\pi(q) = R(q) - C(q)$$

If we want to determine the quantity that maximizes profit, we can differentiate the profit function:

$$d\pi/dq = dR/dq - dC/dq$$

At an interior optimum, the **first-order condition** requires:

$$d\pi/dq = 0$$

Therefore:

$$dR/dq - dC/dq = 0$$

Because the derivative of revenue represents marginal revenue and the derivative of cost represents marginal cost:

$$MR - MC = 0$$

which gives:

MR = MC

This familiar economic relationship can therefore emerge directly from the mathematics of the firm's optimization problem. Instead of merely memorizing that profit maximization is associated with marginal revenue equaling marginal cost under the appropriate conditions, calculus allows us to see why that relationship occurs.

Finding a point where the first derivative equals zero, however, is not necessarily enough to establish that we have found a maximum. A stationary point could also represent a minimum. The **second-order condition** allows us to examine the curvature of the objective function and determine what kind of solution we have found.

This introduces an important principle that will appear throughout the book: economic analysis using calculus is rarely about performing one mathematical operation in isolation. A complete analysis may require us to define the economic objective, construct an appropriate function, differentiate it, solve the resulting condition, evaluate the solution, and then interpret what the answer means economically.

Calculus also allows us to approach another type of economic problem: accumulation.

Suppose we are interested not in the rate of change at a particular point, but in the total amount accumulated across an interval. This leads to

integration, which allows us to work with areas under curves and accumulated quantities. In economics, integration becomes useful for analyzing concepts such as consumer surplus and producer surplus, among other applications.

Throughout the book, calculus will primarily help us:

- Measure economic rates of change.
- Analyze marginal relationships.
- Maximize or minimize economic objectives.
- Determine how economic variables respond to one another.
- Measure accumulated quantities and areas.
- Construct and interpret mathematical economic models.

The objective is not to make economics appear more complicated. The objective is to use mathematics where mathematics allows us to analyze an economic relationship more precisely.

From Economic Theory to Mathematical Models

Economic theory often begins with a description of behavior. Consumers respond to prices and income, firms respond to costs and revenues, workers respond to wages and employment opportunities, and investment decisions respond to expected returns, interest rates, and other economic conditions. These ideas can be discussed verbally, but mathematical analysis requires us to represent the relationships in a more structured form.

Economists therefore use **economic models** to isolate particular relationships and examine them systematically. A model is intentionally simplified. It does not attempt to reproduce every detail of an economy, market, consumer, or business. Instead, it identifies the variables that are important to the question being studied and establishes relationships among them.

Consider demand.

We might begin with the economic idea that, holding other relevant factors constant, quantity demanded generally decreases as the price of a product increases.

We can represent this relationship as:

$$Qd = f(P)$$

This simply states that quantity demanded is a function of price.

A specific demand function might be:

$$Qd = 200 - 5P$$

If:

$P = 10$

then:

$Qd = 200 - 5(10)$

$Qd = 150$

The verbal relationship has now become a mathematical model that can be evaluated at different prices.

More sophisticated models can contain several variables simultaneously. Quantity demanded might depend on the price of the product, consumer income, and the price of a substitute:

$Qd = f(P, Y, Ps)$

where:

- P = price of the product
- Y = consumer income
- Ps = price of a substitute
- Qd = quantity demanded

This type of model recognizes that demand does not exist in isolation. Consumers make decisions in an environment where income, competing products, complementary products, preferences, expectations, and other conditions may also matter.

Mathematical analysis frequently requires us to isolate one of these relationships by **holding other variables constant**. If we want to understand how quantity demanded changes as income changes, for example, we may hold prices constant so that we can focus specifically on the relationship between income and demand.

Suppose:

$$Q = f(Y)$$

Calculus allows us to examine:

$$dQ/dY$$

which measures the rate at which quantity demanded changes with respect to income.

If a model instead contains several independent variables, we can examine the effect of one variable while treating the others as constant. This becomes increasingly important as we move into economic models containing several interacting variables.

The basic analytical process can be summarized as follows:

- Identify the economic question.
- Determine the relevant variables.

- Express the relationship with an appropriate function.
- Identify which variable is changing.
- Apply the appropriate mathematical method.
- Solve the model.
- Interpret the result in economic terms.

That final step is essential.

Suppose an optimization problem produces:

$q^* = 500$

The number 500 means very little until we understand what q represents. It might refer to 500 units of output per day, 500 labor hours, 500 units of capital, or another economic quantity. We also need to understand why 500 is considered optimal and what assumptions produced that result.

The same principle applies to a derivative.

Suppose:

$dQ/dY = 4$

The mathematical answer is 4, but the economic interpretation depends on the units assigned to Q and Y. If Y is measured in thousands of dollars rather than individual dollars, for example, the interpretation changes substantially.

Calculus-based economic analysis therefore requires attention to more than mathematical manipulation. The analyst must keep track of variables, units, assumptions, functional relationships, and economic meaning.

This is one reason mathematical models can be powerful without being perfect representations of reality. A model gives us a controlled environment in which we can study a particular relationship, but its conclusions must always be understood within the assumptions and structure of that model.

As the models become more sophisticated, this distinction becomes increasingly important. A mathematically correct solution can still be economically meaningless if the variables are misunderstood, the units are ignored, or the assumptions of the model are applied incorrectly.

Understanding Functions, Variables, and Economic Relationships

Calculus-based economics depends heavily on functions because functions allow relationships between economic variables to be represented mathematically. Before differentiating, integrating, or optimizing an economic model, we need to understand what the variables represent and how the function connects them.

A **variable** is a quantity that can take different values. Common economic variables include:

- Price
- Quantity
- Income
- Cost
- Revenue
- Profit
- Consumption
- Investment
- Capital
- Labor
- Output
- Utility

A **function** describes how one or more variables are related. For example:

$C = f(q)$

states that cost depends on quantity, while:

$R = f(q)$

states that revenue depends on quantity.

A utility function involving two goods might be written as:

$$U = f(x, y)$$

A production function involving capital and labor might be represented as:

$$Q = f(K, L)$$

Functions give us the structure needed to ask more precise economic questions. Once the relationship has been represented mathematically, calculus can help us determine how that relationship behaves as one or more of its variables change.

Consider:

$$C(q) = 100 + 5q + 0.02q^2$$

Here, total cost C depends on quantity q.

If we differentiate the function:

$$C'(q) = 5 + 0.04q$$

we have transformed a function describing total cost into a function describing the rate at which total cost changes.

At:

$$q = 100$$

we obtain:

$C'(100) = 5 + 0.04(100)$

$C'(100) = 9$

At an output level of 100 units, total cost is increasing at approximately 9 monetary units for an additional unit of output.

This illustrates an important distinction:

- The original function describes the **level** of an economic variable.
- The first derivative describes the **rate of change** of that variable.
- The second derivative describes how the rate of change itself is changing.

These distinctions become particularly important when economic relationships are nonlinear.

Suppose:

$C(q) = 100 + 5q$

Then:

$C'(q) = 5$

The rate of change is constant. Every additional unit of output adds 5 monetary units to total cost within this model.

Now compare that with:

$C(q) = 100 + 5q + 0.02q^2$

The derivative is:

$C'(q) = 5 + 0.04q$

The rate of change is no longer constant. As q increases, the rate at which total cost increases also changes.

Many economically important relationships have this type of nonlinear structure. Additional production may eventually become increasingly expensive, additional consumption may produce progressively smaller increases in satisfaction, and additional units of an input may eventually contribute progressively less additional output.

Calculus gives us a way to analyze these changing relationships instead of relying only on visual inspection of a graph.

If:

$f'(x) > 0$

the function is locally increasing.

If:

$f'(x) < 0$

the function is locally decreasing.

The second derivative provides information about curvature:

$$f''(x) > 0$$

indicates local convexity, while:

$$f''(x) < 0$$

indicates local concavity.

These relationships become particularly important when we begin solving optimization problems. A first derivative can help us locate a candidate optimum, while the second derivative can help us determine whether that candidate represents a maximum or minimum under the conditions of the model.

As the book progresses, the notation and functions will become more involved. We will encounter demand and supply functions, utility functions, production functions, cost and revenue functions, profit functions, growth relationships, and models involving several economic variables. However, the underlying analytical structure will remain consistent.

We will use functions to represent economic relationships, derivatives to examine rates of change, optimization to identify economically significant choices, and integration to measure accumulation and areas associated with economic curves. Understanding that structure now will make the more advanced applications that follow much easier to analyze.

Last Thoughts

Calculus provides a mathematical language for examining some of the most important questions in economics, particularly those involving change, marginal relationships, optimization, and accumulation. The purpose of learning these techniques in an economic context is not simply to become better at manipulating equations, but to understand what the mathematics reveals about economic behavior. Functions allow us to represent relationships, derivatives allow us to measure how those relationships change, optimization allows us to identify economically significant choices, and integration allows us to examine quantities accumulated across intervals. With these foundations established, we can begin examining derivatives and marginal economic analysis in greater depth, while continuing to connect every mathematical calculation to the economic question it is intended to answer.

Chapter 1: Derivatives and Marginal Economic Analysis

Economic analysis becomes more powerful when we move from asking how much of something exists to asking how that quantity changes. A firm may know its total production cost, but determining how rapidly that cost changes as output expands provides additional information for production decisions. A business may know its total revenue, but understanding how revenue changes as sales increase can reveal whether additional output remains worthwhile. These are fundamentally questions about rates of change, and derivatives provide the mathematical tools needed to analyze them. In this chapter, we will examine the economic meaning of derivatives, connect them to marginal cost, marginal revenue, and marginal benefit, and explore how first and second derivatives provide different information about the behavior of economic functions.

Rates of Change and the Economic Meaning of Derivatives

Before focusing on derivatives themselves, it is useful to distinguish between an economic variable's total value and the rate at which that value changes.

Suppose a firm's total production cost increases from \$10,000 to \$10,600 when output increases from 500 units to 520 units. We can calculate the changes as follows:

Change in cost:

\$10,600 - \$10,000 = \$600

Change in output:

520 - 500 = 20

The average change in cost per unit across this interval is therefore:

\$600 / 20 = \$30

This tells us that total cost increased by an average of \$30 for each additional unit produced between 500 and 520 units.

However, this calculation describes an average across an interval. It does not necessarily tell us the rate at which cost is changing precisely at 500 units, 510 units, or 520 units. If the cost relationship is nonlinear, the rate of change itself may vary throughout that interval.

A derivative allows us to examine the rate of change at a particular point.

Consider the total cost function:

$C(q) = 500 + 10q + 0.05q^2$

where q represents output.

To determine how cost changes as output changes, we differentiate the function with respect to q.

The constant term 500 becomes:

0

The derivative of 10q is:

10

Using the power rule, the derivative of $0.05q^2$ is:

$0.10q$

Therefore:

$C'(q) = 10 + 0.10q$

This derivative gives us a new function describing the rate at which total cost changes as output changes.

At:

$q = 100$

we have:

$C'(100) = 10 + 0.10(100)$

$C'(100) = 20$

This means that around an output level of 100 units, total cost is increasing at approximately $20 for an additional unit of output.

It is important to distinguish this result from total cost itself.

Using the original function:

$C(100) = 500 + 10(100) + 0.05(100^2)$

$C(100) = 2{,}000$

At 100 units of production, the model therefore tells us two different things:

- Total cost is $2,000.
- Total cost is increasing at approximately $20 per additional unit around that output level.

The original function gives us the level of cost, while its derivative gives us the rate at which cost is changing.

We can apply the same reasoning to revenue.

Suppose:

$R(q) = 50q - 0.1q^2$

Differentiating gives:

$R'(q) = 50 - 0.2q$

At an output of 100 units:

$R'(100) = 50 - 0.2(100)$

$R'(100) = 30$

Revenue is therefore increasing at approximately $30 for an additional unit of output around $q = 100$.

The usefulness of derivatives becomes even clearer when we compare linear and nonlinear relationships.

Suppose:

$y = 5x + 10$

The derivative is:

$dy/dx = 5$

No matter which value of x we examine, the rate of change remains 5. The relationship has a constant slope.

Now consider:

$y = x^2$

The derivative becomes:

dy/dx = 2x

The rate of change now depends on x.

At x = 2:

dy/dx = 4

At x = 5:

dy/dx = 10

At x = 10:

dy/dx = 20

As x increases, the function becomes increasingly steep. This type of changing rate is common in economic models because economic relationships are not always linear. Costs can rise at an increasing rate, additional benefits can diminish, and the productivity of additional inputs can change as more resources are employed.

Derivatives allow these changing rates to be measured rather than merely observed.

Graphically, the derivative can also be interpreted as the slope of a tangent line at a particular point on a curve. Instead of calculating the average slope between two separated points, calculus allows us to examine the slope at a specific point.

The sign of the derivative provides immediate information about the behavior of the function:

- If $f'(x) > 0$, the function is locally increasing.
- If $f'(x) < 0$, the function is locally decreasing.
- If $f'(x) = 0$, the function is stationary at that point.

These relationships are especially important in economics because a change in the sign of a derivative can indicate that an economic relationship has reached an important turning point. A profit function, for example, may increase while its derivative is positive, reach a stationary point when its derivative becomes zero, and begin decreasing when the derivative becomes negative.

Understanding rates of change therefore provides the foundation for the marginal and optimization analysis that follows.

Marginal Cost, Marginal Revenue, and Marginal Benefit

The connection between derivatives and economic marginal concepts is one of the most important applications of calculus in economics. Marginal quantities describe how a total economic quantity changes as the underlying activity changes.

For a differentiable total cost function:

$C(q)$

the marginal cost function can be represented as:

$MC(q) = C'(q)$

Similarly, if total revenue is:

$R(q)$

then:

$MR(q) = R'(q)$

And if total benefit is:

$B(q)$

then:

$MB(q) = B'(q)$

These relationships allow us to derive marginal functions directly from total functions.

Consider the following total cost function:

$C(q) = 1{,}000 + 20q + 0.02q^2$

Differentiating gives:

$MC(q) = 20 + 0.04q$

At an output of 500 units:

$MC(500) = 20 + 0.04(500)$

$MC(500) = 40$

The firm's marginal cost around an output level of 500 units is therefore approximately $40 per additional unit.

Now suppose the firm's inverse demand function is:

$P(q) = 100 - 0.05q$

Because total revenue equals price multiplied by quantity:

$R(q) = P(q)q$

Substituting the inverse demand function gives:

$R(q) = (100 - 0.05q)q$

Multiplying through:

R(q) = 100q - 0.05q^2

We can now differentiate the revenue function:

$MR(q) = 100 - 0.10q$

At an output of 500 units:

$MR(500) = 100 - 0.10(500)$

MR(500) = 50

At q = 500, the model therefore gives us:

MC = $40

MR = $50

The marginal revenue associated with additional output is greater than the marginal cost. Around this production level, increasing output slightly would add more to revenue than to cost.

Now consider an output level of 700 units.

Marginal cost becomes:

MC(700) = 20 + 0.04(700)

MC(700) = 48

Marginal revenue becomes:

MR(700) = 100 - 0.10(700)

MR(700) = 30

Now:

MR < MC

Around this output level, additional production adds more to cost than it adds to revenue.

The comparison can be summarized as follows:

- When MR > MC, additional output can increase profit at the margin.
- When MR < MC, additional output reduces profit at the margin.
- When MR = MC, the firm has reached an important candidate condition for an interior profit-maximizing quantity.

The same reasoning applies to benefits and costs more broadly.

Suppose the total benefit from an activity is:

$B(x) = 80x - 2x^2$

Differentiating gives:

$MB(x) = 80 - 4x$

The marginal benefit declines as x increases.

Suppose the corresponding total cost function is:

$C(x) = 10x + x^2$

Differentiating gives:

$MC(x) = 10 + 2x$

Marginal cost increases as x increases.

At $x = 5$:

$MB(5) = 80 - 4(5)$

$MB(5) = 60$

while:

$MC(5) = 10 + 2(5)$

$MC(5) = 20$

At this level of activity:

$MB > MC$

The additional benefit is greater than the additional cost.

At $x = 15$:

$MB(15) = 80 - 4(15)$

$MB(15) = 20$

while:

$MC(15) = 10 + 2(15)$

$MC(15) = 40$

Now:

$MB < MC$

The additional cost has become greater than the additional benefit.

We can determine where the two marginal quantities are equal:

$80 - 4x = 10 + 2x$

Subtract 10 from both sides:

$70 - 4x = 2x$

Add 4x to both sides:

$70 = 6x$

Therefore:

$x = 70/6$

x approximately equals 11.67

At approximately 11.67 units of activity:

MB = MC

This relationship is important because it demonstrates how calculus can turn an economic principle into a solvable mathematical condition. Instead of simply observing that additional benefits eventually become smaller while additional costs become larger, we can determine the precise point at which the two marginal relationships intersect within the model.

There is also an important distinction between marginal values derived through calculus and the literal change created by adding one whole unit. A derivative measures an instantaneous rate of change. When economic quantities are modeled as continuous variables, the derivative provides the marginal value at a point and can approximate the effect of a sufficiently small change in quantity.

For example, if:

$$MC(500) = 40$$

we interpret this as total cost increasing at a rate of approximately $40 per additional unit around $q = 500$. The exact cost of moving from 500 units to 501 units would instead be:

$$C(501) - C(500)$$

For many smooth functions and sufficiently small changes, the derivative provides a useful approximation. Recognizing this distinction becomes increasingly important as economic models become more mathematically sophisticated.

Marginal analysis is therefore not merely about attaching the word "marginal" to an economic variable. It involves studying how total economic relationships change at particular points and using those changes to understand incentives, tradeoffs, and decisions.

First and Second Derivatives in Economic Analysis

The first derivative tells us how a function is changing, but economic analysis often requires additional information. We may also want to know whether that rate of change is increasing or decreasing.

This is where the second derivative becomes useful.

Consider:

$f(x) = 12x - x^2$

The first derivative is:

$f'(x) = 12 - 2x$

The second derivative is:

$f''(x) = -2$

The negative second derivative tells us that the function is concave throughout this model.

This information becomes especially important when identifying maxima and minima.

Suppose a firm's profit function is:

$pi(q) = 120q - 2q^2 - 500$

The first derivative is:

$pi'(q) = 120 - 4q$

To locate a stationary point, set the first derivative equal to zero:

$$120 - 4q = 0$$

Solving gives:

$$4q = 120$$

$$q = 30$$

This tells us that $q = 30$ is a candidate stationary point, but the first derivative alone does not yet establish that the point maximizes profit.

Differentiate again:

$$\pi''(q) = -4$$

Because:

$$\pi''(q) < 0$$

the profit function is concave, so the stationary point corresponds to a local maximum.

Within this model, profit is therefore maximized at:

$$q^* = 30$$

This illustrates the different roles played by the first and second derivatives:

- The first derivative helps locate stationary points and describes the direction in which a function is changing.
- The second derivative describes curvature and can help classify a stationary point as a maximum or minimum.

The same relationship can be understood by examining how the sign of the first derivative changes around a stationary point.

For a local maximum, we generally expect:

Positive -> Zero -> Negative

Before the maximum, the function is increasing. At the stationary point, its slope is zero. After the maximum, the function is decreasing.

For a local minimum, the pattern is generally:

Negative -> Zero -> Positive

The function decreases before the stationary point and increases afterward.

The second derivative provides another way to evaluate these situations. At a stationary point, under the usual differentiability conditions:

- If $f''(x) < 0$, the point is a local maximum.
- If $f''(x) > 0$, the point is a local minimum.

- If $f''(x) = 0$, the second derivative test is inconclusive, so additional analysis may be required.

That final condition matters. A second derivative equal to zero does not automatically mean that no maximum or minimum exists. It simply means that this particular test does not provide enough information to classify the stationary point.

Second derivatives can also tell us something economically meaningful even when we are not explicitly solving an optimization problem.

Consider the total cost function:

$C(q) = 1{,}000 + 5q + 0.03q^2$

The first derivative is:

$C'(q) = 5 + 0.06q$

and the second derivative is:

$C''(q) = 0.06$

Because the second derivative is positive, marginal cost increases as output increases.

Now consider a benefit function:

$B(q) = 100q - 0.5q^2$

The first derivative is:

$B'(q) = 100 - q$

and the second derivative is:

$B''(q) = -1$

The negative second derivative tells us that marginal benefit decreases as q increases.

These results give us a useful way to organize the information contained in an economic function:

- The original function describes the total relationship.
- The first derivative describes its marginal behavior.
- The second derivative describes how that marginal behavior is changing.

This layered interpretation is one of the reasons calculus is so valuable in economic analysis. A single mathematical function can contain information about the level of an economic variable, its rate of change, and the way that rate of change evolves as conditions change.

First and second derivatives will therefore appear repeatedly throughout the chapters ahead. We will use them to examine supply and demand relationships, elasticity, optimization, utility, production, costs, revenues, and profit. Although the economic context will change, the mathematical reasoning developed here will remain an important part of each analysis.

Last Thoughts

Derivatives allow economic analysis to move beyond total quantities and examine how economic relationships change at particular points. By differentiating cost, revenue, and benefit functions, we can derive marginal relationships that help explain the incentives behind economic decisions. First derivatives tell us the direction and rate of change of a function, while second derivatives allow us to examine how that rate itself is changing and provide valuable information about curvature, maxima, and minima. These tools become especially powerful when applied to specific economic relationships rather than studied in isolation. In the next chapter, we will build on this foundation by applying derivatives directly to supply, demand, and elasticity, allowing us to examine not only whether economic quantities change, but how responsive they are to changes in prices, income, and other economic variables.

Chapter 2: Supply, Demand, and Elasticity Through Calculus

Supply and demand are often introduced graphically, with an upward-sloping supply curve intersecting a downward-sloping demand curve to determine market equilibrium. That framework remains important, but calculus allows us to investigate these relationships at a deeper level. Instead of looking only at whether quantity demanded or supplied rises or falls, we can measure the rate at which those quantities respond to changes in price, income, and other economic variables. We can also analyze nonlinear demand and supply functions whose slopes change from one point to another and use derivatives to calculate elasticity at specific locations along a curve. These tools allow supply and demand analysis to move from a primarily graphical framework toward a more precise mathematical examination of market behavior.

Building and Analyzing Supply and Demand Functions

A **demand function** represents the relationship between the quantity consumers demand and one or more variables that influence purchasing decisions.

A simple demand function can be written as:

Qd = f(P)

where:

- Qd = quantity demanded
- P = price

Consider the linear demand function:

Qd = 500 - 5P

If the price is $20:

Qd = 500 - 5(20)

Qd = 400

If the price rises to $40:

Qd = 500 - 5(40)

Qd = 300

Within this model, higher prices are associated with lower quantities demanded.

Because the function is linear, its derivative with respect to price is constant:

$dQd/dP = -5$

This means that quantity demanded changes at a rate of negative 5 units for each one-unit increase in price.

The negative sign is economically meaningful. It tells us that price and quantity demanded move in opposite directions within the model.

A supply relationship can be constructed similarly.

Suppose:

$Qs = 50 + 10P$

where Qs represents quantity supplied.

Differentiating with respect to price gives:

$dQs/dP = 10$

The positive derivative indicates that quantity supplied increases as price increases.

At this stage, the derivative might seem unnecessary because the coefficients of linear functions already reveal their slopes. The real power of calculus becomes clearer when the relationships are nonlinear.

Consider:

$Qd = 800 - 4P - 0.1P^2$

Differentiating gives:

$dQd/dP = -4 - 0.2P$

The slope now depends on price.

At:

$P = 10$

the derivative is:

$dQd/dP = -4 - 0.2(10)$

$dQd/dP = -6$

At:

$P = 30$

the derivative becomes:

$dQd/dP = -4 - 0.2(30)$

$dQd/dP = -10$

The demand curve is therefore changing at different rates at different prices. Calculus allows us to measure the slope at each specific point rather than assuming that the relationship has a constant rate of change.

Demand and supply can also be expressed as **inverse functions**, where price is written as a function of quantity.

Instead of:

$$Qd = f(P)$$

we might write:

$$P = f(Qd)$$

For example:

$$P = 100 - 0.2Q$$

This equation tells us the price associated with each quantity demanded.

Differentiating with respect to Q gives:

$$dP/dQ = -0.2$$

An inverse supply function might be:

$$P = 10 + 0.1Q$$

which gives:

$$dP/dQ = 0.1$$

The inverse forms are particularly useful when analyzing revenue, surplus, and optimization because price can be substituted directly into other economic functions.

Supply and demand functions can also be used to determine **market equilibrium**.

Suppose:

$Qd = 500 - 5P$

and:

$Qs = 100 + 5P$

At equilibrium:

$Qd = Qs$

Therefore:

$500 - 5P = 100 + 5P$

Subtract 100:

$400 - 5P = 5P$

Add 5P:

$400 = 10P$

Therefore:

$P^* = 40$

Substitute the equilibrium price into either function:

$Q^* = 500 - 5(40)$

$Q^* = 300$

The equilibrium is therefore:

$P^* = 40$

$Q^* = 300$

Calculus is not required to solve this particular linear equilibrium, but the functions establish the mathematical framework that will allow us to perform more advanced analysis.

Realistic demand models may contain several explanatory variables rather than price alone.

A demand function might take the form:

$$Qd = 1{,}000 - 8P + 0.02Y + 4Ps$$

where:

- P = price of the good
- Y = consumer income
- Ps = price of a substitute

This equation represents several economic relationships simultaneously. Quantity demanded can change because the product's own price changes, because consumer income changes, or because the price of a substitute changes.

To analyze these relationships separately, we need to determine how Qd changes with respect to one variable while holding the others constant. This brings us to a particularly important application of derivatives in economic modeling.

Measuring Changes in Quantity, Price, and Income

When a function depends on several independent variables, economists often need to isolate the effect of one variable while treating the others as constant.

Suppose:

Qd = f(P, Y, Ps)

Quantity demanded depends on price, income, and the price of a substitute.

We may want to answer three different questions:

- How does quantity demanded change when the product's own price changes?
- How does quantity demanded change when consumer income changes?
- How does quantity demanded change when the price of the substitute changes?

Because several independent variables appear in the same function, we can use **partial derivatives** to examine each relationship separately.

Consider:

Qd = 1,000 - 8P + 0.02Y + 4Ps

To determine how quantity demanded responds to the product's own price, differentiate with respect to P while treating Y and Ps as constants:

$\partial Qd/\partial P = -8$

The negative value indicates that quantity demanded decreases as the product's price increases.

Now differentiate with respect to income:

$\partial Qd/\partial Y = 0.02$

This positive value indicates that quantity demanded increases as income increases within this model.

Finally:

$\partial Qd/\partial Ps = 4$

The positive value indicates that demand for the original product increases as the substitute becomes more expensive.

Each derivative provides information about a different economic relationship contained within the same demand function.

The notation is important.

When a function contains one independent variable, we may write:

dQ/dP

When a function contains several independent variables and we differentiate with respect to one while holding the others constant, we commonly use the partial derivative notation:

$\partial Q/\partial P$

This distinction becomes increasingly important as economic models become more complex.

Consider a more detailed example:

$Qd = 2{,}500 - 10P + 0.04Y + 6Ps$

Suppose:

$P = 50$

$Y = 40{,}000$

$Ps = 60$

The quantity demanded is:

$Qd = 2{,}500 - 10(50) + 0.04(40{,}000) + 6(60)$

$Qd = 2{,}500 - 500 + 1{,}600 + 360$

$Qd = 3{,}960$

Now consider the income relationship:

$\partial Qd/\partial Y = 0.04$

This derivative tells us that, holding the other variables constant, quantity demanded changes by 0.04 units for each one-unit increase in the income variable.

Units matter considerably here.

If Y is measured in dollars, the interpretation differs from a model in which Y is measured in thousands of dollars. The derivative itself does not tell us which unit convention was used. That information must come from the definition of the variables.

Suppose instead that Y represents thousands of dollars.

Then:

$\partial Qd/\partial Y = 0.04$

would describe the change in quantity demanded associated with a $1,000 increase in income, not a $1 increase.

This demonstrates why mathematical economic analysis requires careful interpretation in addition to correct differentiation.

Partial derivatives also allow us to distinguish among different types of goods.

Suppose quantity demanded for a good depends on income:

$Q = f(Y)$

If:

$\partial Q/\partial Y > 0$

quantity demanded rises as income rises, which is consistent with a normal good within the relevant range of the model.

If:

$\partial Q/\partial Y < 0$

quantity demanded falls as income rises, which is consistent with an inferior good within that range.

Cross-price relationships can be examined similarly.

Suppose:

$Qx = f(Py)$

where Qx represents demand for good X and Py represents the price of good Y.

If:

$\partial Qx/\partial Py > 0$

an increase in the price of Y increases demand for X, which is consistent with the two goods being substitutes.

If:

$\partial Qx/\partial Py < 0$

an increase in the price of Y decreases demand for X, which is consistent with the goods being complements.

These derivatives provide useful information about the direction and magnitude of economic relationships, but magnitude alone can create a comparison problem.

Suppose one product has:

$dQ/dP = -5$

while another has:

$dQ/dP = -50$

It might appear that the second product is much more responsive to price.

But what if the first product typically sells 10 units at a price of \$2 while the second sells 100,000 units at a price of \$5,000?

The derivatives are expressed in different scales, so comparing them directly can be misleading.

To compare responsiveness across products and markets, economists often need a unit-free measure.

That leads to elasticity.

Calculating and Interpreting Elasticity With Derivatives

Elasticity measures the responsiveness of one economic variable to a change in another. Unlike a simple slope, elasticity expresses responsiveness in proportional or percentage terms, allowing comparisons across variables measured in different units or operating at different scales.

One of the most widely used measures is the **price elasticity of demand**.

For a differentiable demand function:

$Q = Q(P)$

point price elasticity can be written as:

$Ed = (dQ/dP)(P/Q)$

This formula contains two components.

The first:

dQ/dP

measures how quantity demanded changes with respect to price.

The second:

P/Q

converts that rate of change into a proportional measure.

Because ordinary demand curves generally have:

$dQ/dP < 0$

price elasticity of demand is usually negative. Depending on the convention being used, economists may report the negative value directly or discuss elasticity using its absolute value.

Consider:

$Q = 500 - 5P$

The derivative is:

$dQ/dP = -5$

Suppose:

$P = 20$

Then:

$Q = 500 - 5(20)$

$Q = 400$

Substitute these values into the elasticity formula:

$Ed = (-5)(20/400)$

$Ed = (-5)(0.05)$

$Ed = -0.25$

The absolute value is:

$|Ed| = 0.25$

Because:

$|Ed| < 1$

demand is inelastic at this point.

The standard interpretation is:

- $|Ed| > 1$ indicates elastic demand.
- $|Ed| < 1$ indicates inelastic demand.
- $|Ed| = 1$ indicates unit elastic demand.

An elastic demand means the percentage change in quantity demanded is proportionally larger than the percentage change in price. Inelastic demand means the percentage change in quantity demanded is proportionally smaller than the percentage change in price.

Now examine the same demand function at a different price.

Suppose:

$P = 80$

Then:

Q = 500 - 5(80)

Q = 100

The derivative remains:

dQ/dP = -5

But elasticity becomes:

Ed = (-5)(80/100)

Ed = -4

Therefore:

|Ed| = 4

Demand is elastic at this point.

This result reveals an important distinction between slope and elasticity.

The linear demand function:

Q = 500 - 5P

has a constant slope of:

-5

throughout the entire curve.

Its elasticity, however, is not constant.

At $P = 20$, we found:

$Ed = -0.25$

At $P = 80$:

$Ed = -4$

The slope remains identical, but the proportional responsiveness changes because P and Q change as we move along the demand curve.

This is one reason derivatives are so useful in elasticity analysis. They allow us to calculate responsiveness at a specific point rather than relying only on average changes across an interval.

Elasticity can also be calculated for nonlinear demand functions.

Suppose:

$Q = 1{,}000P^{-2}$

Differentiate using the power rule:

$dQ/dP = -2{,}000P^{-3}$

The elasticity formula is:

$Ed = (dQ/dP)(P/Q)$

Substitute the functions:

$Ed = (-2{,}000P^{-3})(P / 1{,}000P^{-2})$

Simplifying gives:

$Ed = -2$

In this case, elasticity is constant even though the demand function itself is nonlinear.

This illustrates another important point: a linear demand curve can have changing elasticity, while certain nonlinear demand functions can have constant elasticity.

Calculus helps us distinguish these properties mathematically.

We can also apply elasticity to income.

The **income elasticity of demand** can be written as:

$Ey = (\partial Q/\partial Y)(Y/Q)$

This measures the percentage responsiveness of quantity demanded to a percentage change in income.

In general:

- $Ey > 0$ is consistent with a normal good.
- $Ey < 0$ is consistent with an inferior good.
- Larger positive values indicate greater responsiveness of demand to income.

Cross-price elasticity can be written as:

$Exy = (\partial Qx/\partial Py)(Py/Qx)$

This measures how demand for good X responds proportionally to a change in the price of good Y.

In general:

- $Exy > 0$ is consistent with substitute goods.
- $Exy < 0$ is consistent with complementary goods.
- Exy near 0 suggests a relatively weak cross-price relationship within the model.

Supply can also be analyzed using elasticity.

For:

$Qs = Qs(P)$

the **price elasticity of supply** can be written as:

$Es = (dQs/dP)(P/Qs)$

Suppose:

$Qs = 100 + 10P$

Then:

$dQs/dP = 10$

At:

$P = 20$

quantity supplied is:

$Qs = 100 + 10(20)$

$Qs = 300$

Therefore:

$Es = (10)(20/300)$

$Es = 200/300$

$Es \approx 0.67$

Supply is inelastic at this point because the proportional change in quantity supplied is smaller than the proportional change in price.

These calculations demonstrate why elasticity provides information that the derivative alone cannot provide. A derivative tells us the rate at which one variable changes with respect to another in the units of the model. Elasticity rescales that relationship so that responsiveness can be interpreted proportionally.

The distinction can be summarized as follows:

- Slope tells us the absolute rate of change.
- Elasticity tells us the proportional responsiveness.

- A derivative allows slope to be measured at a specific point.
- The elasticity formula combines that derivative with the current values of the variables.

Elasticity also has important implications for revenue.

Total revenue is:

$$R = PQ$$

If demand is elastic, a price reduction can increase total revenue because the percentage increase in quantity demanded exceeds the percentage decrease in price. If demand is inelastic, a price reduction can decrease total revenue because quantity demanded does not increase proportionally enough to offset the lower price.

This relationship can also be derived mathematically.

If quantity depends on price:

$$R(P) = P\,Q(P)$$

Differentiate using the product rule:

$$dR/dP = Q + P(dQ/dP)$$

Factor out Q:

$dR/dP = Q[1 + (dQ/dP)(P/Q)]$

Because:

$Ed = (dQ/dP)(P/Q)$

we obtain:

$dR/dP = Q(1 + Ed)$

This equation directly connects price elasticity of demand to changes in total revenue.

If:

$Ed = -1$

then:

$dR/dP = 0$

At unit elasticity, total revenue is stationary with respect to a small change in price.

If demand is elastic:

$Ed < -1$

then:

$1 + Ed < 0$

so:

$dR/dP < 0$

An increase in price reduces total revenue locally, while a decrease in price increases it.

If demand is inelastic:

$-1 < Ed < 0$

then:

$1 + Ed > 0$

so:

$dR/dP > 0$

An increase in price increases total revenue locally, while a decrease in price reduces it.

This is a good example of how calculus allows familiar economic relationships to be derived rather than simply memorized. Demand, elasticity, and revenue are not separate concepts. They are mathematically connected components of the same economic system.

Last Thoughts

Supply and demand functions provide a mathematical framework for representing how markets respond to changing conditions, while calculus allows those relationships to be examined at specific points and across models containing several variables. Derivatives reveal how quantity demanded or supplied changes with price, partial derivatives allow us to isolate the effects of income and related-good prices, and elasticity converts those rates of change into proportional measures that can be compared across different markets and scales. The distinction between slope and elasticity is particularly important because a constant slope does not necessarily imply constant responsiveness. These tools also begin connecting market behavior to economic decision-making, especially when elasticity affects revenue and when changing marginal relationships influence optimal choices. In the next chapter, we will build on these foundations by examining economic optimization more directly, including objective functions, choice variables, first-order conditions, and the mathematical requirements for identifying optimal economic decisions.

Chapter 3: Economic Optimization and Decision-Making

Many economic problems are ultimately choice problems. A consumer must decide how much of a product to purchase, a firm must determine how much output to produce, an investor must allocate limited capital, and a business may need to choose how much labor, equipment, or another input to employ. In each case, the decision-maker is attempting to achieve some objective while facing costs, limitations, or competing alternatives. Calculus provides a systematic framework for analyzing these problems. By constructing an objective function, identifying the relevant choice variable, and examining how the objective changes as that variable changes, we can determine where an economic decision reaches an optimum and whether the resulting solution actually represents the maximum or minimum we are seeking.

Objective Functions and Choice Variables

An **objective function** mathematically represents what a decision-maker is attempting to maximize or minimize.

Depending on the economic problem, an objective might involve:

- Maximizing profit
- Maximizing utility
- Maximizing net benefit
- Maximizing output
- Minimizing production cost
- Minimizing expenditure
- Minimizing another economic loss or burden

Once the objective has been identified, we need to determine the **choice variable**, which is the variable the decision-maker can select or control within the model.

Suppose a firm chooses how much output to produce. Quantity q is the choice variable.

If profit depends on output:

$$\pi(q) = R(q) - C(q)$$

then profit is the objective function and q is the choice variable.

The firm's problem can be expressed as:

$\max \pi(q)$

This notation tells us that the firm is choosing q in an attempt to maximize profit.

Consider:

$R(q) = 100q - q^2$

and:

$C(q) = 20q + 200$

Profit is:

$\pi(q) = R(q) - C(q)$

Substituting the functions gives:

$\pi(q) = 100q - q^2 - 20q - 200$

Simplifying:

$\pi(q) = 80q - q^2 - 200$

We now have an objective function expressed entirely in terms of the firm's choice variable.

Before differentiating, it is useful to understand what this function represents. If the firm chooses a very low output, it may be giving up profitable opportunities to sell additional units. If it chooses an excessively high output, falling revenue at the margin or increasing costs may make additional production undesirable. The optimization problem asks us to identify the quantity that performs best according to the objective represented by the model.

Not every economic objective involves profit.

Suppose an individual receives a benefit from some activity according to:

$$B(x) = 60x - x^2$$

while the associated cost is:

$$C(x) = 12x$$

If the objective is to maximize net benefit, we can construct:

$$NB(x) = B(x) - C(x)$$

Therefore:

$$NB(x) = 60x - x^2 - 12x$$

$$NB(x) = 48x - x^2$$

The decision-maker chooses x to maximize net benefit.

Optimization problems can also involve minimization.

Suppose a cost function is:

$$C(q) = q^2 - 20q + 300$$

If the economic question asks us to determine the quantity associated with the minimum value of this function, the objective becomes:

$$\min C(q)$$

The calculus procedures used to locate candidate maxima and minima are closely related. What changes is the economic interpretation of the objective and the conditions used to classify the solution.

An important part of optimization is therefore translating a verbal economic problem into the appropriate mathematical structure.

Before performing any calculus, it is useful to identify:

- What is the decision-maker trying to accomplish?
- What variable can the decision-maker choose?
- What variables are outside the decision-maker's control?
- What benefits or revenues are associated with the decision?
- What costs or tradeoffs are associated with it?

- Are there constraints limiting the available choices?

This process prevents us from treating optimization as a purely mechanical exercise.

Consider a firm choosing labor input L.

Suppose output is:

$Q(L) = 20L - 0.5L^2$

and the firm receives \$10 for each unit of output while paying a wage of \$50 for each unit of labor.

Revenue generated from output is:

$10Q(L)$

Labor cost is:

$50L$

Profit, ignoring other costs for simplicity, becomes:

$\pi(L) = 10(20L - 0.5L^2) - 50L$

Multiplying through:

$\pi(L) = 200L - 5L^2 - 50L$

Therefore:

$\pi(L) = 150L - 5L^2$

The choice variable is not output in this example. It is labor.

The firm is solving:

max $\pi(L)$

This distinction matters because the derivative must be taken with respect to the variable being chosen.

Economic optimization therefore begins before calculus is performed. We first need to understand the decision, identify the objective, and express the problem in a mathematical form suitable for analysis.

First-Order Conditions and Marginal Benefit Equals Marginal Cost

Once an objective function has been constructed, the next step is often to determine where its slope equals zero.

For an objective:

$F(x)$

a candidate interior optimum may satisfy:

$F'(x) = 0$

This equation is the first-order condition already introduced earlier in the book.

To understand why this condition matters, consider a function that increases as x rises, eventually reaches a peak, and then begins decreasing.

Before the peak:

$F'(x) > 0$

At the peak:

$F'(x) = 0$

After the peak:

$F'(x) < 0$

The zero derivative identifies the point where the function stops increasing and begins decreasing.

Return to our profit function:

$\pi(q) = 80q - q^2 - 200$

Differentiate with respect to q:

$\pi'(q) = 80 - 2q$

Set the derivative equal to zero:

$80 - 2q = 0$

Therefore:

$2q = 80$

$q^* = 40$

The asterisk is commonly used to indicate an optimal or candidate optimal value.

We can also see this condition through marginal revenue and marginal cost.

Because:

$\pi(q) = R(q) - C(q)$

differentiate both sides:

$\pi'(q) = R'(q) - C'(q)$

Since:

$R'(q) = MR(q)$

and:

$C'(q) = MC(q)$

we obtain:

$\pi'(q) = MR(q) - MC(q)$

At an interior stationary point:

$\pi'(q) = 0$

Therefore:

$MR - MC = 0$

and:

$MR = MC$

The profit-maximization condition emerges from the derivative of the profit function.

A similar relationship appears when the objective is net benefit.

Suppose:

$NB(x) = B(x) - C(x)$

Differentiate:

$NB'(x) = B'(x) - C'(x)$

Because the derivatives represent marginal benefit and marginal cost:

$NB'(x) = MB(x) - MC(x)$

At an interior stationary point:

$NB'(x) = 0$

Therefore:

$MB - MC = 0$

which gives:

MB = MC

This condition has a clear economic interpretation.

Suppose:

MB > MC

An additional amount of the activity generates more additional benefit than additional cost. Increasing the activity can therefore raise net benefit locally.

If:

MB < MC

the additional cost exceeds the additional benefit. Increasing the activity further reduces net benefit locally.

At an interior optimum:

MB = MC

the two marginal effects balance.

Consider:

B(x) = 80x - 2x^2

and:

C(x) = 20x + x^2

Net benefit is:

$NB(x) = B(x) - C(x)$

$NB(x) = 80x - 2x^2 - 20x - x^2$

$NB(x) = 60x - 3x^2$

Differentiate:

$NB'(x) = 60 - 6x$

Set the first derivative equal to zero:

$60 - 6x = 0$

Therefore:

$x^* = 10$

We can obtain the same answer by comparing the marginal functions.

Marginal benefit is:

$MB(x) = 80 - 4x$

Marginal cost is:

$MC(x) = 20 + 2x$

Set them equal:

$80 - 4x = 20 + 2x$

Subtract 20:

$60 - 4x = 2x$

Therefore:

$60 = 6x$

$x^* = 10$

The two approaches are mathematically equivalent because net benefit is defined as total benefit minus total cost.

We can also evaluate what happens around the candidate optimum.

At $x = 8$:

$MB(8) = 80 - 4(8)$

$MB(8) = 48$

$MC(8) = 20 + 2(8)$

$MC(8) = 36$

Therefore:

$MB > MC$

Increasing the activity remains beneficial at the margin.

At $x = 12$:

$MB(12) = 80 - 4(12)$

$MB(12) = 32$

$MC(12) = 20 + 2(12)$

$MC(12) = 44$

Therefore:

$MB < MC$

The activity has moved beyond the point where additional benefits justify additional costs.

At $x = 10$:

$MB(10) = 40$

$MC(10) = 40$

The marginal quantities are equal.

This interpretation is more useful than simply memorizing MB = MC. It explains the economic forces that push the decision toward the optimum.

The same reasoning can be applied to our labor example:

$\pi(L) = 150L - 5L^2$

Differentiate:

$\pi'(L) = 150 - 10L$

Set the derivative equal to zero:

$150 - 10L = 0$

Therefore:

$L^* = 15$

Within the model, the candidate profit-maximizing labor input is 15 units.

However, an important qualification is necessary. Setting the derivative equal to zero identifies a stationary point, but not every optimum must satisfy this equation.

If the optimum occurs at the boundary of the feasible set, the derivative may not equal zero there. Similarly, a function may contain stationary points that are not maxima or minima.

For that reason, solving the first-order condition is an important step, but it is not always the final step.

Second-Order Conditions, Concavity, and Optimal Solutions

After finding a candidate stationary point, we need to determine what kind of point we have found.

This is where the second derivative becomes particularly useful.

Suppose:

$F'(x^*) = 0$

If:

$F''(x^*) < 0$

the function is locally concave at the stationary point, which supports identifying x* as a local maximum.

If:

$F''(x^*) > 0$

the function is locally convex at the stationary point, which supports identifying x* as a local minimum.

If:

$F''(x^*) = 0$

the second derivative test is inconclusive, and another method may be needed.

Return to the profit function:

$\pi(q) = 80q - q^2 - 200$

We found:

$\pi'(q) = 80 - 2q$

and:

$q^* = 40$

Differentiate again:

$\pi''(q) = -2$

Because:

$\pi''(40) = -2 < 0$

the profit function is concave, and $q = 40$ represents a local maximum.

We can verify the economic meaning by calculating profit around the optimum.

At $q = 30$:

$\pi(30) = 80(30) - 30^2 - 200$

$\pi(30) = 2{,}400 - 900 - 200$

$\pi(30) = 1{,}300$

At $q = 40$:

$\pi(40) = 80(40) - 40^2 - 200$

$\pi(40) = 3{,}200 - 1{,}600 - 200$

$\pi(40) = 1{,}400$

At $q = 50$:

$\pi(50) = 80(50) - 50^2 - 200$

$\pi(50) = 4,000 - 2,500 - 200$

$\pi(50) = 1,300$

Profit rises as output approaches 40 units and falls after output moves beyond 40 units.

Now consider a minimization problem:

$C(q) = q^2 - 20q + 300$

Differentiate:

$C'(q) = 2q - 20$

Set the first derivative equal to zero:

$2q - 20 = 0$

Therefore:

$q^* = 10$

Now differentiate again:

$C''(q) = 2$

Because:

$C''(10) > 0$

the function is convex at the stationary point, indicating a minimum.

The distinction between concavity and convexity is therefore economically useful.

For a maximization problem, a concave objective function has a shape consistent with a peak. For a minimization problem, a convex objective function has a shape consistent with a valley.

In simple one-variable problems, the second derivative test can make this classification straightforward. More complicated economic models may require additional methods, but the underlying logic remains important.

We should also distinguish between a **local optimum** and a **global optimum**.

A local maximum is greater than nearby values of the function. A global maximum is greater than or equal to every other feasible value of the function.

Similarly, a local minimum is lower than nearby values, while a global minimum is lower than or equal to every other feasible value.

This distinction matters because some economic functions can contain several peaks and valleys.

Suppose an objective function contains two local maxima. Solving the first-order condition may identify both of them, but the decision-maker ultimately wants the one producing the highest attainable value if the goal is global maximization.

For well-behaved concave objective functions over convex feasible sets, optimization can be much simpler because a local maximum can also be the global maximum. This is one reason assumptions about the shape of economic functions matter.

Boundaries must also be considered.

Suppose a decision-maker can choose:

$$0 <= x <= 10$$

and the objective function continues increasing throughout that entire interval.

There may be no interior point satisfying:

$$F'(x) = 0$$

The optimum could instead occur at:

$$x = 10$$

The economic analyst should therefore not automatically assume that every optimization problem can be solved by differentiating and setting the derivative equal to zero.

A more complete procedure is:

- Define the objective function.
- Identify the choice variable.

- Identify any constraints or feasible boundaries.
- Differentiate the objective with respect to the choice variable.
- Solve the first-order condition for interior candidates.
- Use the second derivative or another appropriate method to classify candidates.
- Check relevant boundary values when necessary.
- Compare feasible candidates if more than one exists.
- Interpret the optimal solution economically.

Consider a constrained choice where:

$0 \le x \le 20$

and:

$F(x) = 30x - x^2$

Differentiate:

$F'(x) = 30 - 2x$

Set equal to zero:

$30 - 2x = 0$

$x^* = 15$

Because 15 lies within the feasible interval, it is a valid interior candidate.

The second derivative is:

$F''(x) = -2$

Therefore, x = 15 is a local maximum.

Because this quadratic function is concave throughout the feasible interval, that interior maximum is also the global maximum over the interval.

Now change the constraint to:

$0 <= x <= 10$

The unconstrained stationary point remains:

$x^* = 15$

but x = 15 is no longer feasible.

Within the allowable range, the function is still increasing as x approaches 10:

$F'(10) = 30 - 2(10)$

$F'(10) = 10 > 0$

The constrained optimum therefore occurs at the boundary:

$x^* = 10$

This demonstrates an important economic lesson. The mathematically preferred unconstrained choice may not be available to the decision-maker. Budgets, production capacity, available time, regulations, resource limitations, and other constraints can alter the optimal solution.

Optimization is therefore not simply about finding where a derivative equals zero. It is about identifying the best feasible decision within the structure of an economic model.

The first-order condition tells us where an interior candidate may exist. The second-order condition helps us understand the shape of the objective around that candidate. Concavity and convexity provide information about the broader structure of the function, while constraints determine which choices are actually available.

Together, these concepts provide a foundation for increasingly sophisticated economic optimization.

Last Thoughts

Economic optimization brings together many of the calculus concepts developed so far by placing them inside a decision-making framework. An objective function tells us what is being maximized or minimized, while the choice variable identifies what the decision-maker can control. First-order conditions allow us to locate candidate interior solutions and reveal why important economic rules such as marginal benefit equaling marginal cost emerge naturally from optimization. Second-order conditions, concavity, convexity, and boundary analysis then help determine whether a candidate actually represents the optimal feasible choice. These principles apply across economics, but the objective and constraints change depending on the decision being studied. In the next chapter, we will apply this optimization framework to consumer choice, where individuals allocate limited resources among goods in an attempt to achieve the greatest possible utility.

Chapter 4: Consumer Choice and Utility Optimization

Consumers constantly make decisions about how to allocate limited resources among competing wants. Economic theory represents these decisions by examining the satisfaction consumers receive from different combinations of goods and the financial constraints that limit what they can purchase. Calculus allows this framework to become much more precise. Instead of simply stating that consumers prefer more satisfaction or that they face limited budgets, we can construct utility functions, calculate marginal utility, represent budget constraints mathematically, and determine which affordable combination of goods maximizes utility. Consumer optimization also introduces an important feature of economic calculus: the best decision is often determined not by examining one variable independently, but by comparing the marginal benefits obtained from several competing uses of the same limited resource.

Utility Functions and Marginal Utility

A **utility function** represents a consumer's preferences mathematically by assigning numerical values to different combinations of goods. The numerical value itself does not necessarily represent a measurable amount of happiness. Instead, utility functions are commonly used to rank bundles according to the consumer's preferences.

Suppose a consumer chooses between two goods, X and Y. A utility function can be written as:

$U = U(X,Y)$

where:

- U = utility
- X = quantity of good X
- Y = quantity of good Y

A simple example is:

$U(X,Y) = XY$

If the consumer has:

$X = 4$

and:

$Y = 5$

then:

$U(4,5) = (4)(5)$

$U = 20$

Another bundle might contain:

$X = 2$

$Y = 8$

which gives:

$U(2,8) = (2)(8)$

$U = 16$

Under this particular utility representation, the first bundle is ranked above the second because it produces the higher utility value.

Calculus becomes useful when we want to determine how utility changes as consumption of one good changes while the quantity of another good is held constant.

Because utility depends on more than one variable, we use partial derivatives.

For:

$U(X,Y) = XY$

the partial derivative with respect to X is:

$\partial U/\partial X = Y$

The partial derivative with respect to Y is:

$\partial U/\partial Y = X$

These derivatives represent the marginal utilities of the two goods.

We can write:

$MUx = \partial U/\partial X$

and:

$MUy = \partial U/\partial Y$

At the bundle:

$X = 4$

$Y = 5$

we obtain:

$MUx = 5$

and:

$MUy = 4$

The interpretation is that, around this consumption bundle and holding the other good constant, utility changes at a rate of 5 utility units with respect to X and 4 utility units with respect to Y.

The important idea is not simply that consumers receive utility from goods. Calculus allows us to examine the additional utility associated with changing consumption.

Consider a different utility function:

$U(X,Y) = X^{(1/2)}Y^{(1/2)}$

Differentiate with respect to X:

$MUx = (1/2)X^{(-1/2)}Y^{(1/2)}$

Differentiate with respect to Y:

$MUy = (1/2)X^{(1/2)}Y^{(-1/2)}$

These marginal utilities depend on the quantities already being consumed.

Suppose:

$X = 4$

$Y = 9$

Then:

$MUx = (1/2)(4)^{(-1/2)}(9)^{(1/2)}$

$MUx = (1/2)(1/2)(3)$

$MUx = 0.75$

For Y:

MUy = (1/2)(4)^(1/2)(9)^(-1/2)

MUy = (1/2)(2)(1/3)

MUy = 1/3

These derivatives tell us how utility responds locally to changes in each good.

Many utility functions are constructed to reflect **diminishing marginal utility**, meaning that as consumption of a good increases, the additional utility associated with more of that good decreases, holding other relevant factors constant.

Consider a one-good utility function:

U(X) = 10X^(1/2)

The first derivative is:

U'(X) = 5X^(-1/2)

or:

MUx = 5/sqrt(X)

As X increases, marginal utility decreases.

At:

X = 1

MUx = 5

At:

$X = 4$

$MUx = 2.5$

At:

$X = 25$

$MUx = 1$

Utility itself is still increasing, but it is increasing at a decreasing rate.

This distinction is important. Diminishing marginal utility does not mean that consuming more of the good necessarily reduces total utility. It means that the additional utility obtained from another small increase becomes smaller.

We can see this through the second derivative:

U''(X) = -(5/2)X^(-3/2)

For positive X:

$U''(X) < 0$

The utility function is concave.

This connects consumer theory to the optimization principles developed in the previous chapter. Concavity often provides the curvature needed for a stationary solution to represent a maximum rather than a minimum.

When two goods are involved, marginal utility also helps us understand the tradeoff between them.

The **marginal rate of substitution** measures the rate at which a consumer is willing to substitute one good for another while remaining on the same utility level.

For two goods, its magnitude can be represented by:

$MRS_{xy} = MU_x/MU_y$

Using:

$U(X,Y) = X^{(1/2)}Y^{(1/2)}$

we found:

$MU_x = (1/2)X^{(-1/2)}Y^{(1/2)}$

and:

$MU_y = (1/2)X^{(1/2)}Y^{(-1/2)}$

Taking the ratio gives:

$MRS_{xy} = Y/X$

The consumer's willingness to trade between the two goods therefore depends on the bundle currently being consumed.

If the consumer has a large amount of Y relative to X, an additional amount of X may be relatively valuable at the margin. As the composition of the bundle changes, the marginal tradeoff changes as well.

This relationship becomes central once prices and income are introduced because consumers cannot simply choose whichever bundle produces the greatest utility without considering its cost.

Budget Constraints and Consumer Choice

A consumer generally faces limited income and positive prices. The **budget constraint** represents the combinations of goods the consumer can afford.

Suppose the consumer purchases goods X and Y.

Let:

Px = price of X

Py = price of Y

I = income available for spending

The budget constraint is:

$P_xX + P_yY \le I$

If the consumer spends the entire available budget, the relationship becomes:

$PxX + PyY = I$

Suppose:

$I = \$120$

$Px = \$10$

$Py = \$5$

Then:

$10X + 5Y = 120$

This equation represents all combinations of X and Y that exactly exhaust the consumer's $120 budget.

If the consumer spends everything on X:

$10X = 120$

$X = 12$

If the consumer spends everything on Y:

$5Y = 120$

$Y = 24$

The consumer can also choose combinations between these endpoints.

For example:

$X = 6$

$Y = 12$

costs:

$10(6) + 5(12)$

$= 60 + 60$

$= 120$

and therefore lies on the budget line.

We can rearrange the budget equation to express Y as a function of X:

$5Y = 120 - 10X$

$Y = 24 - 2X$

The slope of the budget line is:

-2

More generally, rearranging:

$P_xX + P_yY = I$

gives:

$Y = I/P_y - (P_x/P_y)X$

The slope is therefore:

$-Px/Py$

This slope represents the market tradeoff between the two goods. If $Px/Py = 2$, obtaining one additional unit of X requires giving up two units of Y while remaining on the same budget line.

The budget constraint therefore introduces scarcity directly into the mathematical model. The consumer may prefer bundles containing large amounts of both goods, but only affordable bundles are feasible.

Several changes can alter the budget constraint.

If income increases while prices remain constant, the consumer can afford more combinations of goods. The intercepts expand outward.

If income decreases, the affordable set contracts.

If the price of X changes while income and the price of Y remain constant, the maximum affordable quantity of X changes, altering the slope of the budget line.

For example, suppose income remains:

$I = 120$

and:

$Py = 5$

but the price of X falls from:

$Px = 10$

to:

$Px = 6$

The new budget constraint becomes:

$6X + 5Y = 120$

If all income is spent on X:

$X = 20$

instead of 12.

The consumer's feasible choices have changed even though income has not.

This illustrates an important aspect of consumer optimization. Preferences tell us what consumers would like, while the budget constraint determines what they can afford. The optimal choice emerges from the interaction of the two.

The mathematical problem can therefore be written as:

maximize $U(X,Y)$

subject to:

$PxX + PyY = I$

The phrase "subject to" is important. The consumer is not maximizing utility over every imaginable combination of X and Y. The maximization takes place only among feasible bundles satisfying the budget constraint.

One way to work with a simple two-good problem is to substitute the budget constraint directly into the utility function.

Suppose:

$U(X,Y) = XY$

with:

$10X + 5Y = 120$

Solve the constraint for Y:

$Y = 24 - 2X$

Substitute this expression into the utility function:

$U(X) = X(24 - 2X)$

Therefore:

$U(X) = 24X - 2X^2$

The original constrained two-variable problem has now been converted into a one-variable optimization problem.

We can differentiate:

$U'(X) = 24 - 4X$

Set the derivative equal to zero:

$24 - 4X = 0$

Therefore:

$X^* = 6$

Substitute $X = 6$ into the budget constraint:

$10(6) + 5Y = 120$

$60 + 5Y = 120$

$5Y = 60$

$Y^* = 12$

The candidate optimal bundle is therefore:

$(X^*, Y^*) = (6,12)$

Notice that this is the same affordable bundle examined earlier, but now we have a mathematical reason for identifying it as significant. It emerges from the consumer's utility-maximization problem.

Maximizing Utility With Calculus

Substitution works well for some simple consumer problems, but calculus provides a more general framework for constrained optimization.

One particularly important technique is the **Lagrange multiplier method**.

Suppose the consumer wants to:

maximize U(X,Y)

subject to:

PxX + PyY = I

We can construct a Lagrangian:

L = U(X,Y) + lambda[I - PxX - PyY]

Here, lambda is a multiplier associated with the budget constraint.

Consider again:

U(X,Y) = XY

subject to:

10X + 5Y = 120

The Lagrangian is:

L = XY + lambda(120 - 10X - 5Y)

We now differentiate with respect to each choice variable and the multiplier.

With respect to X:

$\partial L/\partial X = Y - 10\text{lambda} = 0$

With respect to Y:

$\partial L/\partial Y = X - 5\text{lambda} = 0$

With respect to lambda:

$\partial L/\partial \text{lambda} = 120 - 10X - 5Y = 0$

The first two conditions give:

Y = 10lambda

and:

X = 5lambda

Divide the first relationship by the second:

Y/X = 10/5

Therefore:

Y/X = 2

so:

Y = 2X

Substitute this relationship into the budget constraint:

$10X + 5(2X) = 120$

$10X + 10X = 120$

$20X = 120$

$X^* = 6$

Therefore:

$Y^* = 12$

We obtain the same solution as before.

The value of the Lagrange approach becomes clearer when we examine the economic meaning of the first-order conditions.

From:

Y = 10lambda

and:

X = 5lambda

remember that for U = XY:

$MUx = Y$

$MUy = X$

Therefore:

MUx = lambda Px

and:

MUy = lambda Py

Dividing each marginal utility by its corresponding price gives:

MUx/Px = lambda

MUy/Py = lambda

Therefore, at an interior optimum:

MUx/Px = MUy/Py

This is a fundamental condition for consumer optimization.

It tells us that the marginal utility obtained per monetary unit spent should be equal across the goods at an interior optimum.

Suppose instead:

MUx/Px > MUy/Py

The consumer is obtaining more additional utility per dollar spent on X than on Y. Under the assumptions of the model, shifting some expenditure toward X and away from Y can increase utility.

If:

$MUx/Px < MUy/Py$

the consumer obtains more marginal utility per dollar from Y, creating an incentive to shift spending toward Y.

At an interior optimum:

$MUx/Px = MUy/Py$

there is no marginal gain from reallocating a small amount of expenditure between the two goods.

This condition can also be written as:

$MUx/MUy = Px/Py$

The left side is the consumer's marginal rate of substitution between the goods. The right side is the market price ratio.

Therefore:

$MRSxy = Px/Py$

At an interior utility-maximizing solution, the consumer's marginal willingness to trade between the goods equals the tradeoff imposed by market prices.

Consider a more advanced utility function:

$U(X,Y) = X^{(1/2)}Y^{(1/2)}$

subject to:

$4X + 2Y = 100$

The marginal utilities are:

$MUx = (1/2)X^{(-1/2)}Y^{(1/2)}$

and:

$MUy = (1/2)X^{(1/2)}Y^{(-1/2)}$

At an interior optimum:

$MUx/MUy = Px/Py$

We previously found:

$MUx/MUy = Y/X$

The price ratio is:

$Px/Py = 4/2 = 2$

Therefore:

$Y/X = 2$

so:

$Y = 2X$

Substitute into the budget constraint:

$4X + 2(2X) = 100$

$4X + 4X = 100$

$8X = 100$

$X^* = 12.5$

Then:

$Y^* = 25$

Check the budget:

$4(12.5) + 2(25)$

$= 50 + 50$

$= 100$

The entire budget is allocated.

The resulting bundle is:

$(X^*,Y^*) = (12.5,25)$

We can also evaluate the utility level:

$U(12.5,25) = (12.5)^{(1/2)}(25)^{(1/2)}$

which is approximately:

$U = 17.68$

The exact numerical utility value is less important than the fact that this bundle satisfies the consumer's optimality condition within the model.

There is also an economic interpretation of lambda.

In many constrained optimization problems, the Lagrange multiplier can be interpreted as the marginal value of relaxing the constraint. In this consumer problem, lambda can represent the approximate increase in maximized utility associated with an additional unit of income, under the assumptions of the model.

For the earlier example:

U = XY

with:

X* = 6

Y* = 12

we had:

X = 5lambda

Therefore:

6 = 5lambda

lambda = 1.2

The multiplier indicates the marginal value of additional budget resources in terms of the utility representation being used.

This interpretation makes the Lagrange multiplier more than a mathematical device. It can provide information about how valuable an additional unit of a constrained resource is at the optimum.

However, the interior solution should not automatically be assumed in every consumer problem.

Consumers may choose **corner solutions**, where the optimal bundle contains zero units of one of the goods. This can happen when the marginal benefits relative to prices never produce an interior equality within the feasible set.

The analyst must therefore consider:

- The shape of the utility function
- The consumer's income
- The prices of the goods
- The feasible consumption set
- Whether the calculated solution satisfies the constraints
- Whether an interior solution actually exists

Consumer optimization is therefore another example of the broader principle developed in the previous chapter. Calculus helps identify candidate optimal choices, but economic reasoning is necessary to determine whether those choices are feasible and meaningful.

The consumer problem also demonstrates why multivariable calculus becomes important in economics. Real decisions rarely involve changing only one thing while everything else is irrelevant. Consumers choose among competing goods, firms choose among inputs, and investors choose among assets. Partial derivatives and constrained optimization allow these simultaneous tradeoffs to be represented mathematically.

Last Thoughts

Consumer choice demonstrates how calculus can transform an intuitive economic problem into a structured optimization model. Utility functions represent preferences, marginal utilities describe how utility changes as consumption changes, and budget constraints define the combinations of goods that are financially feasible. By combining these elements, calculus allows us to identify consumption bundles that maximize utility and to derive the important condition that marginal utility per unit of expenditure should be equal across goods at an interior optimum. The Lagrange multiplier method extends this analysis by allowing constraints to be incorporated directly into the optimization problem and by revealing the marginal value of relaxing those constraints. In the next chapter, we will move from consumers to firms, applying similar mathematical reasoning to production functions, costs, revenues, and the determination of profit-maximizing output.

Chapter 5: Production, Costs, Revenue, and Profit

Firms transform inputs such as labor, capital, materials, technology, and energy into goods and services, but the economic value of that production depends on more than the amount of output created. Managers and analysts also need to understand how output changes when inputs change, how costs behave as production expands, how additional sales affect revenue, and where the relationship between revenue and cost produces the greatest profit. Calculus connects these questions through a common mathematical framework. Production functions can be differentiated to measure marginal product, cost and revenue functions can be differentiated to obtain their marginal counterparts, and these relationships can then be combined to determine an optimal level of output. This allows us to examine the firm not simply as a producer, but as an economic decision-maker attempting to allocate resources efficiently within the conditions represented by its model.

Production Functions and Marginal Product

A **production function** describes the relationship between the inputs used by a firm and the output those inputs produce.

A general production function involving labor and capital can be written as:

$Q = f(L,K)$

where:

- Q = quantity of output
- L = labor input
- K = capital input

This function tells us that output depends on the amounts of labor and capital employed.

Because more than one independent variable appears in the function, partial derivatives allow us to isolate the effect of changing one input while holding the other constant.

The marginal product of labor is:

MPL = partial Q / partial L

The marginal product of capital is:

MPK = partial Q / partial K

These derivatives tell us how rapidly output changes when a particular input changes at the margin.

Consider the production function:

$Q = 10L^{(1/2)}K^{(1/2)}$

Differentiate with respect to labor:

$MPL = 5L^{(-1/2)}K^{(1/2)}$

Differentiate with respect to capital:

$MPK = 5L^{(1/2)}K^{(-1/2)}$

Suppose the firm currently uses:

$L = 25$

$K = 100$

The marginal product of labor is:

$MPL = 5(25)^{(-1/2)}(100)^{(1/2)}$

$MPL = 5(1/5)(10)$

$MPL = 10$

At this combination of inputs, output is increasing at a rate of approximately 10 units for an additional unit of labor, holding capital constant.

The marginal product of capital is:

$MPK = 5(25)^{(1/2)}(100)^{(-1/2)}$

$MPK = 5(5)(1/10)$

$MPK = 2.5$

Holding labor constant, output is increasing at a rate of approximately 2.5 units for an additional unit of capital.

These values should not automatically be interpreted as meaning labor is "better" than capital. The inputs may have different prices, units, and roles within production. An economically meaningful comparison must consider what each input costs in addition to what it contributes to output.

Production functions can also help us examine **diminishing marginal product**.

Suppose capital is fixed and output depends on labor according to:

$Q(L) = 40L + 6L^2 - 0.2L^3$

Differentiate:

$MPL = 40 + 12L - 0.6L^2$

The marginal product itself changes as labor changes.

To determine how marginal product changes, differentiate again:

$d(MPL)/dL = 12 - 1.2L$

When:

$12 - 1.2L > 0$

marginal product is increasing.

Solving:

$12 > 1.2L$

$L < 10$

Within this portion of the model, marginal product rises as labor increases.

When:

$L > 10$

the second derivative becomes negative, meaning marginal product begins declining.

This does not necessarily mean total output immediately begins falling. It means each additional unit of labor contributes less additional output than the previous one.

For example, at:

$L = 12$

MPL = 40 + 12(12) - 0.6(12^2)

MPL = 40 + 144 - 86.4

MPL = 97.6

Marginal product remains positive, so additional labor is still increasing total output. However, marginal product is already declining because:

12 - 1.2(12) = -2.4

This distinction is important:

- Positive marginal product means additional input increases total output.
- Declining marginal product means the additional output contributed by successive input increases is becoming smaller.
- Negative marginal product means additional input actually reduces total output within the model.

The mathematical distinction allows us to examine diminishing returns more precisely than simply observing that production eventually becomes less efficient.

Production analysis can also involve tradeoffs between inputs.

Suppose a firm wants to maintain a particular level of output while changing its combination of labor and capital. The **marginal rate of technical**

substitution describes the rate at which one input can substitute for another while maintaining the same output level.

Its magnitude can be represented as:

MRTS = MPL / MPK

For:

$Q = 10L^{(1/2)}K^{(1/2)}$

we found:

$MPL = 5L^{(-1/2)}K^{(1/2)}$

and:

$MPK = 5L^{(1/2)}K^{(-1/2)}$

Taking the ratio gives:

MRTS = K/L

At:

L = 25

K = 100

MRTS = 100/25

MRTS = 4

The marginal productivity tradeoff between labor and capital therefore depends on the firm's existing input combination.

This becomes especially important when input prices are introduced. A firm does not generally want the input combination that simply produces the highest marginal product. It wants to consider productivity relative to the cost of obtaining each input.

Calculus therefore gives production theory a framework for examining both the contribution of individual inputs and the tradeoffs involved in combining them.

Cost and Revenue Functions Through Calculus

Production decisions create costs, while sales generate revenue. Understanding how these quantities change with output is essential for determining whether expanding or reducing production improves the firm's economic position.

A total cost function can generally be written as:

$C(q)$

where q represents output.

Total cost may contain both fixed and variable components.

Consider:

$$C(q) = 2{,}000 + 20q + 0.05q^2$$

The constant:

$$2{,}000$$

represents a fixed cost within the model because it does not change with output.

The remaining terms:

$$20q + 0.05q^2$$

represent costs that vary with production.

Differentiate the total cost function:

$$MC(q) = 20 + 0.10q$$

This gives the marginal cost function.

At:

$$q = 100$$

$$MC(100) = 20 + 0.10(100)$$

$$MC(100) = 30$$

At an output level of 100 units, total cost is increasing at approximately \$30 per additional unit.

At:

$q = 300$

$MC(300) = 20 + 0.10(300)$

$MC(300) = 50$

Marginal cost has increased to approximately \$50.

The second derivative is:

$C''(q) = 0.10$

Because it is positive, marginal cost rises as output increases throughout this particular model.

Notice that the fixed cost disappears when we differentiate:

$d(2{,}000)/dq = 0$

This has an important economic interpretation. Fixed cost affects total profit, but it does not affect the marginal cost of producing an additional unit when the fixed cost truly remains unchanged with output.

Revenue depends on both quantity sold and the price received.

If a firm sells every unit at a constant price P, total revenue is:

$R(q) = Pq$

Suppose:

$P = 60$

Then:

$R(q) = 60q$

and:

$MR(q) = 60$

Marginal revenue is constant because each additional unit adds $60 to total revenue.

However, many economic models assume that the firm faces a downward-sloping demand curve. In that case, selling additional units may require a lower price.

Suppose the inverse demand function is:

$P(q) = 100 - 0.1q$

Total revenue is:

$R(q) = P(q)q$

Therefore:

$R(q) = (100 - 0.1q)q$

$R(q) = 100q - 0.1q^2$

Differentiate:

$MR(q) = 100 - 0.2q$

Marginal revenue now decreases as output increases.

At:

$q = 100$

$MR(100) = 100 - 0.2(100)$

$MR(100) = 80$

At:

$q = 300$

$MR(300) = 100 - 0.2(300)$

$MR(300) = 40$

This declining marginal revenue occurs because increasing quantity affects revenue through both quantity and price.

The distinction becomes clearer if we differentiate revenue before multiplying everything out.

Since:

$R(q) = P(q)q$

the product rule gives:

$R'(q) = P(q) + qP'(q)$

Therefore:

$MR = P + q(dP/dq)$

This equation shows that marginal revenue contains two components:

- Revenue received from the additional quantity sold.
- The revenue effect associated with the price change required by the demand relationship.

For a downward-sloping inverse demand curve:

$dP/dq < 0$

so:

$q(dP/dq) < 0$

and marginal revenue lies below price for positive q.

Using:

$P(q) = 100 - 0.1q$

we have:

$dP/dq = -0.1$

Therefore:

$MR = (100 - 0.1q) + q(-0.1)$

$MR = 100 - 0.2q$

which matches our earlier result.

Average values can also be derived from total functions.

Average cost is:

$AC(q) = C(q)/q$

Using:

$C(q) = 2{,}000 + 20q + 0.05q^2$

we obtain:

$AC(q) = 2{,}000/q + 20 + 0.05q$

Average cost therefore depends on both the spreading of fixed cost across output and the behavior of variable cost.

Differentiate average cost:

$AC'(q) = -2{,}000/q^2 + 0.05$

To find a stationary point:

$-2{,}000/q^2 + 0.05 = 0$

Therefore:

$0.05 = 2{,}000/q^2$

Multiply by q^2:

$0.05q^2 = 2{,}000$

$q^2 = 40{,}000$

For positive output:

$q = 200$

At $q = 200$:

$AC(200) = 2{,}000/200 + 20 + 0.05(200)$

$AC(200) = 10 + 20 + 10$

$AC(200) = 40$

Now calculate marginal cost at the same quantity:

$MC(200) = 20 + 0.10(200)$

$MC(200) = 40$

Therefore:

$MC = AC$

at the minimum of this average cost function.

This relationship can be understood intuitively. When marginal cost is below average cost, the additional unit pulls the average downward. When marginal cost is above average cost, the additional unit pushes the average upward. The minimum occurs where marginal cost crosses average cost.

Calculus allows us to derive these relationships directly from the firm's cost functions rather than relying only on diagrams.

Profit Maximization and Optimal Output

Profit combines the firm's revenue and cost relationships into a single objective.

The **profit function** is:

pi(q) = R(q) - C(q)

The firm chooses output in an attempt to maximize this function, subject to the assumptions and constraints represented by the model.

Suppose inverse demand is:

P(q) = 100 - 0.1q

As derived above:

R(q) = 100q - 0.1q^2

Suppose total cost is:

C(q) = 2,000 + 20q + 0.05q^2

Profit becomes:

pi(q) = (100q - 0.1q^2) - (2,000 + 20q + 0.05q^2)

Simplify:

pi(q) = 80q - 0.15q^2 - 2,000

Differentiate:

pi'(q) = 80 - 0.30q

Set the first derivative equal to zero:

80 - 0.30q = 0

Therefore:

0.30q = 80

q* = 80/0.30

q* approximately equals 266.67

This is the candidate profit-maximizing output.

We can obtain the same result by equating marginal revenue and marginal cost.

Marginal revenue is:

MR(q) = 100 - 0.2q

Marginal cost is:

MC(q) = 20 + 0.1q

Set:

MR = MC

Therefore:

100 - 0.2q = 20 + 0.1q

Subtract 20:

80 - 0.2q = 0.1q

Add 0.2q:

80 = 0.3q

Therefore:

q* approximately equals 266.67

The two approaches produce the same result because:

pi'(q) = MR(q) - MC(q)

At the candidate optimum:

pi'(q) = 0

which implies:

MR = MC

We should now verify the second-order condition.

Differentiate the profit function again:

$pi''(q) = -0.30$

Because:

$pi''(q) < 0$

the profit function is concave, confirming that the stationary point is a local maximum.

We can also determine the price associated with the optimal quantity.

The inverse demand function is:

$P(q) = 100 - 0.1q$

Substitute:

$q^* = 266.67$

$P^* = 100 - 0.1(266.67)$

P^* approximately equals 73.33

The model therefore produces an optimal combination of approximately:

$q^* = 266.67$

$P^* = \$73.33$

Now calculate total revenue:

R(266.67) approximately equals:

73.33(266.67)

R approximately equals $19,555.56

Total cost is:

C(266.67) = 2,000 + 20(266.67) + 0.05(266.67^2)

C approximately equals $10,888.98

Profit is therefore approximately:

pi = 19,555.56 - 10,888.98

pi approximately equals $8,666.58

Minor differences can occur from rounding intermediate values.

The mathematical solution is useful, but its economic interpretation is more important. Below the optimal output, marginal revenue exceeds marginal cost, so additional production contributes positively to profit at the margin. Beyond the optimum, marginal cost exceeds marginal revenue, so additional production reduces profit.

The logic can be summarized as:

- MR > MC: increasing output raises profit locally.
- MR < MC: increasing output lowers profit locally.

- MR = MC: the firm reaches a candidate interior profit-maximizing quantity.

However, the equality MR = MC should not be applied mechanically without considering the surrounding conditions.

Suppose marginal revenue equals marginal cost at a point where the profit function is locally convex rather than concave. The stationary point could represent a minimum rather than a maximum.

Similarly, a firm's feasible production range may prevent it from reaching the unconstrained optimum.

Suppose the model indicates:

$q^* = 266.67$

but the firm's current production capacity is limited to:

$q <= 200$

The unconstrained optimum is not feasible.

We would then need to evaluate the firm's objective over the feasible range. If profit is still increasing at $q = 200$, the constrained optimum may occur at the production-capacity boundary.

Production decisions can also be framed in terms of inputs rather than output.

Suppose a firm's production depends on labor:

Q(L)

and output sells at price P.

If labor costs w per unit, profit might be:

pi(L) = P Q(L) - wL - F

where F represents fixed cost.

Differentiate with respect to labor:

dpi/dL = P(dQ/dL) - w

Because:

dQ/dL = MPL

the first-order condition becomes:

P(MPL) - w = 0

Therefore:

P(MPL) = w

The expression:

P(MPL)

is the value of the additional output generated by an additional unit of labor under a constant output price assumption.

The firm expands labor use while the value created by additional labor exceeds its wage cost and reduces labor use when the wage exceeds the value of the additional output. At an interior optimum under the assumptions of the model, the two become equal.

This demonstrates that the same optimization structure can appear at different levels of firm decision-making.

For output:

$$MR = MC$$

For a simplified labor decision:

$$P(MPL) = w$$

More generally, the firm compares the marginal contribution of a decision with its marginal cost.

This principle connects production, cost, revenue, and profit into a unified mathematical framework. Production functions describe how inputs create output, cost functions describe the resources sacrificed to produce it, revenue functions describe the income generated from selling it, and the profit function combines these relationships into an objective that can be optimized.

Calculus allows each layer of this process to be examined separately and then connected to the others.

Last Thoughts

Production and profit analysis demonstrate how several mathematical relationships can work together within a single economic decision. Production functions allow us to measure the marginal contribution of labor, capital, and other inputs, while cost and revenue functions show how the financial consequences of production change as output expands. Differentiating these functions produces marginal product, marginal cost, and marginal revenue, which can then be used to evaluate whether additional inputs or output improve the firm's objective. Profit maximization brings these relationships together through the condition that marginal revenue equals marginal cost at an appropriate interior optimum, while second-order conditions and feasibility constraints help determine whether that solution is actually optimal. In the next chapter, we will move from differentiation to integration and examine how calculus can measure accumulated economic quantities and areas, including consumer and producer surplus.

Chapter 6: Integration and Economic Surplus

Differentiation allows economists to examine how an economic quantity changes at a particular point, while integration allows us to examine how quantities accumulate across an interval. This distinction makes integration especially useful when the economic question involves totals that are represented by areas beneath or between curves. Consumer surplus and producer surplus are two important examples. Instead of approximating these areas with simple geometric shapes, integration allows us to calculate them directly from demand and supply functions, including nonlinear functions for which ordinary triangle formulas may no longer be sufficient. Understanding integration therefore expands our ability to move between marginal relationships and total economic quantities.

Definite Integrals and Areas Under Economic Curves

An integral can be thought of as a process of accumulation. If differentiation begins with a function and determines its rate of change, integration can often begin with a rate and recover information about the accumulated quantity.

Suppose marginal cost is:

$MC(q) = 10 + 0.2q$

Because marginal cost represents the derivative of total cost:

$MC(q) = C'(q)$

we can integrate the marginal cost function to recover the variable portion of total cost:

$C(q) = \text{integral } (10 + 0.2q)\, dq$

Integrating term by term gives:

$C(q) = 10q + 0.1q^2 + F$

where F is a constant.

Economically, this constant may represent fixed cost because differentiating a constant produces zero, causing fixed cost to disappear from the marginal cost function.

If we know that:

$C(0) = 500$

then:

$500 = 10(0) + 0.1(0)^2 + F$

Therefore:

$F = 500$

and the complete total cost function is:

$C(q) = 500 + 10q + 0.1q^2$

This relationship demonstrates how differentiation and integration work in opposite directions.

Starting with:

$C(q) = 500 + 10q + 0.1q^2$

differentiation gives:

$MC(q) = 10 + 0.2q$

Starting with the marginal function and integrating gives:

$C(q) = 10q + 0.1q^2 + F$

The constant must then be determined from additional information.

When an integral includes this unspecified constant, it is called an **indefinite integral**.

Economic analysis frequently requires a different type of integral, however. Instead of finding a general antiderivative, we may want to determine the amount accumulated between two particular values.

This requires a **definite integral**.

Suppose we want to determine the increase in variable cost as production expands from 100 units to 200 units.

Using:

MC(q) = 10 + 0.2q

we calculate:

integral from 100 to 200 of (10 + 0.2q) dq

The antiderivative is:

10q + 0.1q^2

Evaluate it at the upper and lower limits:

[10q + 0.1q^2] from 100 to 200

At q = 200:

10(200) + 0.1(200^2)

= 2,000 + 4,000

= 6,000

At q = 100:

10(100) + 0.1(100^2)

= 1,000 + 1,000

= 2,000

Therefore:

6,000 - 2,000 = 4,000

The accumulated increase in variable cost between 100 and 200 units is $4,000.

This can also be confirmed using the total cost function.

C(200) = 500 + 10(200) + 0.1(200^2)

C(200) = 6,500

C(100) = 500 + 10(100) + 0.1(100^2)

C(100) = 2,500

Therefore:

C(200) - C(100) = 4,000

The integral of marginal cost over the interval gives the change in total cost.

This relationship generalizes:

C(b) - C(a) = integral from a to b of MC(q) dq

The same idea can be applied to other marginal functions. Integrating marginal revenue across an interval can provide the corresponding change in total revenue, while integrating another marginal quantity can recover its accumulated change when the necessary mathematical conditions are satisfied.

Definite integrals also have a geometric interpretation.

If:

$y = f(x)$

then:

integral from a to b of f(x) dx

represents the signed area between the function and the horizontal axis over the interval from a to b.

If the function remains above the horizontal axis, this corresponds to the ordinary area under the curve.

For example, suppose:

$f(x) = 2x + 4$

and we want the area from:

$x = 0$

to:

$x = 5$

We calculate:

integral from 0 to 5 of (2x + 4) dx

The antiderivative is:

$x^2 + 4x$

Evaluate:

$[x^2 + 4x]$ from 0 to 5

$= (25 + 20) - 0$

$= 45$

The area under the function over that interval is 45 square units.

In economics, however, the units represented by an integral depend on the variables involved. When price is measured vertically and quantity horizontally, integrating price with respect to quantity produces monetary units because:

price x quantity = monetary value

This is precisely why integration is useful for calculating economic surplus.

The general process is:

- Identify the function representing the relevant boundary.
- Determine the interval over which accumulation occurs.
- Construct the definite integral.
- Find the antiderivative.

- Evaluate it at the upper and lower limits.
- Interpret the result using the economic units of the model.

The ability to calculate areas directly from functions becomes particularly valuable when curves are nonlinear.

Calculating Consumer Surplus

Consumer surplus measures the difference between what consumers are willing to pay for units of a good and what they actually pay.

Graphically, consumer surplus is represented by the area below the demand curve and above the market price, up to the quantity purchased.

Suppose inverse demand is:

$P(q) = 100 - 0.5q$

and the market price is:

$P^* = 40$

First determine the quantity demanded at that price:

$40 = 100 - 0.5q$

Subtract 100:

$-60 = -0.5q$

Therefore:

$q^* = 120$

Consumers purchase 120 units at a market price of $40.

The demand curve represents willingness to pay for successive units. At lower quantities, consumers are willing to pay more than $40 for the corresponding marginal units. However, the market price remains $40.

Consumer surplus is therefore:

CS = integral from 0 to 120 of [P(q) - P*] dq

Substitute the functions:

CS = integral from 0 to 120 of [(100 - 0.5q) - 40] dq

Simplify:

CS = integral from 0 to 120 of (60 - 0.5q) dq

The antiderivative is:

60q - 0.25q^2

Evaluate from 0 to 120:

CS = [60q - 0.25q^2] from 0 to 120

At q = 120:

60(120) - 0.25(120^2)

= 7,200 - 3,600

= 3,600

Therefore:

CS = $3,600

Because this demand function is linear, we could also calculate consumer surplus using the area formula for a triangle.

The vertical distance between the demand intercept and market price is:

100 - 40 = 60

The quantity is:

120

Therefore:

CS = (1/2)(120)(60)

CS = $3,600

The two methods produce the same result.

If the triangle formula works, why use calculus?

Because not every demand curve is linear.

Consider a nonlinear inverse demand function:

$P(q) = 100 - q^2$

Suppose the market price is:

$P^* = 36$

Determine the quantity demanded:

$36 = 100 - q^2$

$q^2 = 64$

For nonnegative quantity:

$q^* = 8$

Consumer surplus becomes:

CS = integral from 0 to 8 of $[(100 - q^2) - 36]$ dq

Simplify:

CS = integral from 0 to 8 of $(64 - q^2)$ dq

The antiderivative is:

$64q - q^3/3$

Evaluate:

CS = $[64q - q^3/3]$ from 0 to 8

$CS = 64(8) - 8^3/3$

CS = 512 - 512/3

CS = 1024/3

Therefore:

CS approximately equals $341.33

The area is curved, so treating it as an ordinary triangle would produce the wrong result.

Integration allows the area to be calculated from the actual demand function.

There is another useful way to understand consumer surplus.

The integral:

integral from 0 to q* of P(q) dq

represents the total willingness to pay for the quantity q* under the demand interpretation of the model.

Actual expenditure is:

P*q*

Therefore:

CS = integral from 0 to q* of P(q) dq - P*q*

For our first example:

integral from 0 to 120 of (100 - 0.5q) dq

gives:

[100q - 0.25q^2] from 0 to 120

= 12,000 - 3,600

= 8,400

Actual expenditure is:

40(120) = 4,800

Therefore:

CS = 8,400 - 4,800

CS = 3,600

This interpretation shows that consumer surplus is the difference between the area representing total willingness to pay and the rectangle representing actual expenditure.

The calculus formulation therefore provides both a computational method and a way to understand the economic meaning of the area.

Calculating Producer Surplus

Producer surplus measures the difference between the amount producers receive for units sold and the minimum amounts represented by the supply curve for supplying those units.

Graphically, producer surplus is the area above the supply curve and below the market price, up to the quantity sold.

Suppose inverse supply is:

$P(q) = 10 + 0.25q$

and the market price is:

$P^* = 40$

First determine the quantity supplied:

$40 = 10 + 0.25q$

Subtract 10:

$30 = 0.25q$

Therefore:

$q^* = 120$

Producer surplus is:

PS = integral from 0 to 120 of [P* - P(q)] dq

Substitute:

PS = integral from 0 to 120 of [40 - (10 + 0.25q)] dq

Simplify:

PS = integral from 0 to 120 of (30 - 0.25q) dq

The antiderivative is:

30q - 0.125q^2

Evaluate from 0 to 120:

PS = [30q - 0.125q^2] from 0 to 120

At q = 120:

30(120) - 0.125(120^2)

= 3,600 - 1,800

= 1,800

Therefore:

PS = $1,800

Because the supply curve is linear, we can verify this using the triangle formula.

The market price is $40 and the vertical intercept of supply is $10, giving a height of:

40 - 10 = 30

The base is:

120

Therefore:

PS = (1/2)(120)(30)

PS = $1,800

As with consumer surplus, integration becomes more important when the supply curve is nonlinear.

Suppose:

P(q) = 10 + q^2

and the market price is:

P* = 74

Determine the quantity supplied:

74 = 10 + q^2

q^2 = 64

Therefore:

q* = 8

Producer surplus becomes:

PS = integral from 0 to 8 of [74 - (10 + q^2)] dq

Simplify:

PS = integral from 0 to 8 of (64 - q^2) dq

The antiderivative is:

$64q - q^3/3$

Evaluate:

$PS = 64(8) - 8^3/3$

$PS = 512 - 512/3$

$PS = 1024/3$

Therefore:

PS approximately equals $341.33

Again, integration allows us to calculate the area associated with a curved supply function directly.

Producer surplus can also be expressed as total revenue minus the area under the supply curve.

Total revenue at the market price is:

P*q*

The area under the supply curve is:

integral from 0 to q* of P(q) dq

Therefore:

PS = P*q* - integral from 0 to q* of P(q) dq

Using our linear example:

$P^* = 40$

$q^* = 120$

Total revenue is:

$40(120) = 4{,}800$

Now calculate the area under supply:

integral from 0 to 120 of (10 + 0.25q) dq

The antiderivative is:

10q + 0.125q^2

Evaluate:

10(120) + 0.125(120^2)

= 1,200 + 1,800

= 3,000

Therefore:

PS = 4,800 - 3,000

PS = $1,800

Consumer and producer surplus can also be analyzed together at market equilibrium.

Suppose demand is:

$Pd(q) = 100 - 0.5q$

and supply is:

$Ps(q) = 10 + 0.25q$

At equilibrium:

$Pd(q) = Ps(q)$

Therefore:

$100 - 0.5q = 10 + 0.25q$

Subtract 10:

$90 - 0.5q = 0.25q$

Add 0.5q:

$90 = 0.75q$

Therefore:

$q^* = 120$

Substitute into either function:

$P^* = 40$

This gives the same market price and quantity used in our earlier calculations.

Consumer surplus is:

$3,600

Producer surplus is:

$1,800

Total surplus is therefore:

TS = CS + PS

TS = 3,600 + 1,800

TS = $5,400

We can also calculate total surplus directly as the area between demand and supply from zero to the equilibrium quantity:

TS = integral from 0 to 120 of [Pd(q) - Ps(q)] dq

Substitute:

TS = integral from 0 to 120 of [(100 - 0.5q) - (10 + 0.25q)] dq

Simplify:

TS = integral from 0 to 120 of (90 - 0.75q) dq

The antiderivative is:

90q - 0.375q^2

Evaluate:

$TS = 90(120) - 0.375(120^2)$

$TS = 10{,}800 - 5{,}400$

$TS = \$5{,}400$

The result is exactly equal to consumer surplus plus producer surplus.

This calculation demonstrates how integration can bring several economic relationships together. Demand represents willingness to pay, supply represents the modeled marginal willingness to accept or marginal cost relationship, and the area between the two curves represents gains from trade within the framework.

It also shows why integration is more than a mathematical method for calculating geometric areas. The areas themselves represent economically meaningful quantities.

Last Thoughts

Integration gives economic analysis a way to move from marginal relationships toward accumulated quantities and to measure areas that have direct economic interpretations. Definite integrals can calculate changes in total quantities from their marginal functions, while areas beneath and between economic curves allow consumer surplus, producer surplus, and total surplus to be measured precisely. For linear functions, these calculations may sometimes be reproduced with simple geometry, but integration becomes particularly valuable when demand, supply, cost, or other economic relationships are nonlinear. The broader lesson is that differentiation and integration are closely connected: differentiation examines what happens at the margin, while integration allows those marginal changes to be accumulated across an interval. In the next chapter, we will extend calculus beyond individual consumers, firms, and markets and examine how rates of change can be used to analyze macroeconomic relationships involving growth, capital, investment, and changes through time.

Chapter 7: Calculus in Macroeconomic Analysis

Macroeconomics examines economic activity at an aggregate level, including national output, investment, capital accumulation, consumption, employment, and economic growth. Many of these variables are inherently dynamic because their values change through time. Calculus provides a natural language for studying these movements. A derivative can measure the instantaneous growth of output, investment can be interpreted as a rate of change in the capital stock, and differential relationships can describe how important macroeconomic variables evolve together. The mathematics therefore allows us to move beyond comparing economic values at two separate dates and instead analyze the processes generating economic change. In this chapter, we will examine economic growth as a rate-of-change problem, explore the relationship between capital and investment, and use functions and calculus to analyze broader macroeconomic relationships.

Economic Growth and Rates of Change

Suppose the level of real economic output is represented by:

$Y(t)$

where:

Y = real output

t = time

If we know output at two points in time, we can calculate an average change over the interval. Suppose real output increases from $1 trillion to $1.05 trillion during one year.

The absolute change is:

Delta Y = 1.05 - 1.00

Delta Y = 0.05 trillion

The proportional change is:

Delta Y / Y = 0.05 / 1.00

= 0.05

or 5 percent.

This familiar calculation measures growth across a discrete interval. Calculus allows us to consider what happens when time is treated as continuous.

The derivative:

dY/dt

measures the instantaneous rate at which output changes with respect to time.

If:

$dY/dt > 0$

output is increasing at that moment.

If:

$dY/dt < 0$

output is decreasing.

If:

$dY/dt = 0$

output is momentarily stationary.

However, the absolute rate of change alone does not tell us how large the change is relative to the size of the economy. An economy producing $10 trillion and growing by $100 billion per year is in a different proportional position from an economy producing $1 trillion and growing by the same $100 billion.

We can therefore define the **instantaneous growth rate** as:

$$gY = (1/Y)(dY/dt)$$

or equivalently:

$gY = Y'(t)/Y(t)$

This expresses the rate of change in output relative to the current level of output.

If:

$Y = 2{,}000$

and:

$dY/dt = 60$

then:

$gY = 60/2{,}000$

$gY = 0.03$

which corresponds to an instantaneous growth rate of:

3 percent

This distinction between absolute and proportional change appears throughout macroeconomic analysis.

Consider an exponential output function:

$Y(t) = Y0e^{(gt)}$

where:

Y0 = initial output

g = constant continuous growth parameter

t = time

Differentiate:

dY/dt = gY0e^(gt)

Because:

Y(t) = Y0e^(gt)

we can write:

dY/dt = gY

Divide both sides by Y:

(1/Y)(dY/dt) = g

The proportional growth rate is constant.

Suppose:

Y(t) = 1,000e^(0.02t)

Then:

dY/dt = 20e^(0.02t)

At:

t = 0

output is:

$$Y(0) = 1{,}000$$

and:

$$dY/dt = 20$$

At that moment, output is increasing at a rate of 20 units per year.

The proportional growth rate is:

$$20/1{,}000 = 0.02$$

or 2 percent.

At:

$$t = 10$$

output becomes:

$$Y(10) = 1{,}000e^{(0.2)}$$

which is approximately:

$$Y(10) = 1{,}221.40$$

The absolute rate of change at that time is:

$$dY/dt = 0.02(1{,}221.40)$$

dY/dt approximately equals 24.43

The economy is now adding more output per year in absolute terms, even though its proportional growth rate remains 2 percent.

This is an important feature of exponential growth. A constant percentage growth rate does not imply a constant absolute increase.

Calculus also gives us a useful relationship involving logarithms.

For a positive variable Y(t):

$$d \ln(Y)/dt = (1/Y)(dY/dt)$$

Therefore:

$$d \ln(Y)/dt = gY$$

The derivative of the natural logarithm of a positive variable with respect to time equals its instantaneous proportional growth rate.

This makes logarithms especially useful when analyzing continuously changing economic variables.

Growth relationships can also be combined.

Suppose aggregate output depends on capital and labor:

$$Y = F(K,L)$$

where:

K = capital

L = labor

If both capital and labor change through time, then output also changes.

For a specific production function such as:

$Y = AK^{\alpha} L^{\beta}$

Y = AK^alpha L^beta

we can take natural logarithms:

ln Y = ln A + alpha ln K + beta ln L

Differentiate with respect to time:

(1/Y)(dY/dt) = (1/A)(dA/dt) + alpha(1/K)(dK/dt) + beta(1/L)(dL/dt)

Using growth-rate notation:

gY = gA + alpha gK + beta gL

This relationship decomposes output growth into contributions associated with changes in productivity, capital, and labor within the model.

The result demonstrates why calculus is useful in macroeconomics. Instead of merely observing that output changed, we can construct mathematical relationships describing how several changing variables contribute to that movement.

Capital, Investment, and Changes Over Time

One of the clearest macroeconomic applications of calculus involves the relationship between investment and the capital stock.

The **capital stock** represents productive assets available at a particular point in time. These may include machinery, structures, equipment, and other productive capital represented within the model.

We can write capital as:

K(t)

Investment contributes to the capital stock, while depreciation reduces it.

A basic capital accumulation equation is:

dK/dt = I(t) - delta K(t)

where:

- K(t) = capital stock
- I(t) = gross investment
- delta = depreciation rate
- delta K(t) = depreciation

This equation says that the rate of change in the capital stock equals gross investment minus depreciation.

Suppose an economy has:

K = 1,000

gross investment of:

I = 100

and a depreciation rate of:

delta = 0.06

Depreciation is:

delta K = 0.06(1,000)

delta K = 60

Therefore:

dK/dt = 100 - 60

dK/dt = 40

The capital stock is increasing at a rate of 40 units per period at that moment.

Several possible relationships follow directly from the equation:

- If I > delta K, the capital stock increases.

- If $I < \delta K$, the capital stock decreases.
- If $I = \delta K$, the capital stock remains stationary at that moment.

This illustrates how a macroeconomic concept can be expressed naturally as a differential equation.

Suppose investment is proportional to output:

$$I(t) = sY(t)$$

where s represents the portion of output devoted to investment.

Then:

$$dK/dt = sY(t) - \delta K(t)$$

If output itself depends on capital:

$$Y = F(K)$$

we can substitute the production function:

$$dK/dt = sF(K) - \delta K$$

Now the evolution of capital depends on the amount of output generated by the existing capital stock, the portion devoted to investment, and depreciation.

Consider the simplified production relationship:

$$Y = 20\sqrt{K}$$

with:

s = 0.25

and:

delta = 0.05

Then investment is:

I = 0.25(20sqrt(K))

I = 5sqrt(K)

The capital accumulation equation becomes:

dK/dt = 5sqrt(K) - 0.05K

Suppose:

K = 400

Then:

dK/dt = 5sqrt(400) - 0.05(400)

dK/dt = 5(20) - 20

dK/dt = 80

Capital is increasing at a rate of 80 units per period.

Now suppose:

K = 10,000

Then:

$$dK/dt = 5\text{sqrt}(10{,}000) - 0.05(10{,}000)$$

$$dK/dt = 5(100) - 500$$

$$dK/dt = 0$$

At this capital level, investment exactly offsets depreciation.

We can determine this stationary capital level algebraically by setting:

$$dK/dt = 0$$

Therefore:

$$5\text{sqrt}(K) - 0.05K = 0$$

For positive K:

$$5\text{sqrt}(K) = 0.05K$$

Divide by 0.05:

$$100\text{sqrt}(K) = K$$

Let:

$$x = \text{sqrt}(K)$$

Then:

$$K = x^2$$

so:

$100x = x^2$

For positive x:

$x = 100$

Therefore:

$K^* = 10{,}000$

This is a **steady state** of the simplified capital accumulation equation because the capital stock does not change when the economy is at that level.

The concept should be interpreted carefully. A steady state does not necessarily mean that every economic variable is zero or that no economic activity occurs. In this example, investment and depreciation continue to occur, but their effects on the capital stock exactly offset one another.

We can also examine the direction of adjustment around the steady state.

At:

$K = 2{,}500$

we have:

$dK/dt = 5(50) - 0.05(2{,}500)$

$dK/dt = 250 - 125$

dK/dt = 125

Capital increases.

At:

K = 22,500

we have:

dK/dt = 5(150) - 0.05(22,500)

dK/dt = 750 - 1,125

dK/dt = -375

Capital decreases.

Within this model, capital moves upward when it is below the steady state and downward when it is sufficiently above it.

Calculus therefore allows macroeconomic analysis to address not only the value of capital at one point, but also the direction in which the system is evolving.

Using Functions and Calculus to Analyze Macroeconomic Relationships

Macroeconomic variables rarely operate independently. Consumption depends on income, investment may depend on interest rates or expected returns, tax revenue depends on economic activity and tax structures, and output depends on combinations of productive inputs. Functions allow these relationships to be represented mathematically, while calculus allows us to determine how changes in one variable affect another.

Consider a consumption function:

C = C(Y)

where:

C = consumption

Y = income

The derivative:

dC/dY

measures how consumption changes as income changes.

In macroeconomics, this derivative can represent the **marginal propensity to consume** within a differentiable consumption model.

Suppose:

C(Y) = 200 + 0.75Y - 0.0001Y^2

Differentiate:

$$dC/dY = 0.75 - 0.0002Y$$

The responsiveness of consumption to income changes with the income level.

At:

$$Y = 1{,}000$$

$$dC/dY = 0.75 - 0.0002(1{,}000)$$

$$dC/dY = 0.55$$

At:

$$Y = 2{,}000$$

$$dC/dY = 0.75 - 0.0002(2{,}000)$$

$$dC/dY = 0.35$$

Within this model, consumption remains positively related to income over this range, but its marginal response declines as income increases.

Macroeconomic relationships can also involve several independent variables.

Suppose investment depends on output and the interest rate:

$$I = I(Y,r)$$

where:

r = interest rate

A particular function might be:

I = 100 + 0.1Y - 500r

We can use partial derivatives to isolate each relationship.

With respect to output:

partial I / partial Y = 0.1

Holding the interest rate constant, investment increases as output increases.

With respect to the interest rate:

partial I / partial r = -500

Holding output constant, investment decreases as the interest rate increases within this model.

The numerical interpretation depends on how r is measured. If r is represented as a decimal, a change from 0.04 to 0.05 is a change of 0.01 rather than 1. This illustrates again why units and variable definitions must be considered when interpreting derivatives.

Macroeconomic models may also involve identities connecting several sectors of the economy.

A simplified expenditure representation of aggregate output can be written as:

$Y = C + I + G + NX$

where:

- C = consumption
- I = investment
- G = government purchases
- NX = net exports

If these variables change through time, differentiating both sides gives:

$$dY/dt = dC/dt + dI/dt + dG/dt + dNX/dt$$

This equation states that the rate of change in aggregate output is related to the rates of change in its expenditure components within the identity.

The result is straightforward, but it demonstrates an important feature of calculus. Once an economic relationship has been represented mathematically, we can analyze not only the levels of its variables but also their rates of change.

Consider another macroeconomic relationship involving government revenue.

Suppose tax revenue depends on income:

$$T = T(Y)$$

A simple proportional tax function might be:

$T(Y) = 0.20Y$

Then:

$dT/dY = 0.20$

Each additional unit of income increases tax revenue by 0.20 units within the model.

A nonlinear tax function might instead be:

$T(Y) = 0.10Y + 0.00002Y^2$

Differentiate:

$dT/dY = 0.10 + 0.00004Y$

The marginal tax relationship now changes with income.

At:

$Y = 1{,}000$

$dT/dY = 0.10 + 0.00004(1{,}000)$

$dT/dY = 0.14$

At:

$Y = 5{,}000$

$dT/dY = 0.10 + 0.00004(5{,}000)$

$dT/dY = 0.30$

The mathematical structure allows the marginal relationship to vary as the level of income changes.

Functions can also be combined through the chain rule.

Suppose consumption depends on disposable income:

$$C = C(Yd)$$

and disposable income depends on total income:

$$Yd = Y - T(Y)$$

We may want to know how consumption changes with respect to total income.

Using the chain rule:

$$dC/dY = (dC/dYd)(dYd/dY)$$

Because:

$$Yd = Y - T(Y)$$

we have:

$$dYd/dY = 1 - dT/dY$$

Therefore:

$$dC/dY = (dC/dYd)(1 - dT/dY)$$

This expression connects the marginal response of consumption to disposable income with the way taxation changes disposable income as total income changes.

Suppose:

$dC/dYd = 0.8$

and:

$dT/dY = 0.25$

Then:

$dC/dY = 0.8(1 - 0.25)$

$dC/dY = 0.8(0.75)$

$dC/dY = 0.60$

Consumption therefore changes at a rate of 0.60 units with respect to an additional unit of total income within this simplified model.

This type of analysis demonstrates how calculus can trace economic effects through interconnected relationships rather than examining each equation separately.

The same reasoning can become considerably more sophisticated. Macroeconomic models may contain simultaneous equations, expectations, dynamic adjustment, differential equations, and multiple state and control variables. The purpose here is not to develop all of those techniques, but to establish the mathematical logic underlying them.

When working with a macroeconomic model, it is useful to ask:

- Which variables represent economic levels?
- Which variables change through time?
- Which variables depend on other variables?
- What does the first derivative represent economically?
- Are proportional growth rates more informative than absolute changes?
- Does the model contain an accumulation process?
- Is there a stationary or steady-state condition?
- How do changes in one relationship transmit into another?

These questions help prevent calculus from becoming detached from economic interpretation.

A derivative such as:

dK/dt

is not simply a mathematical symbol. It represents the rate at which the capital stock changes.

A derivative such as:

dY/dt

represents the rate at which output changes.

A ratio such as:

$(1/Y)(dY/dt)$

represents an instantaneous proportional growth rate.

A condition such as:

$dK/dt = 0$

can identify a stationary capital stock within a dynamic model.

Once these mathematical expressions are connected to their economic meanings, calculus becomes a framework for understanding how aggregate economic systems evolve rather than simply a method for manipulating equations.

Last Thoughts

Macroeconomic analysis extends calculus into an environment where time, growth, and accumulation become central to the economic questions being studied. Derivatives allow us to distinguish between the level of output and its rate of growth, while proportional derivatives provide a natural way to analyze continuously changing growth rates. Capital accumulation demonstrates how differential equations can represent dynamic economic processes, with investment adding to productive capacity while depreciation reduces it and steady-state conditions identifying points where those forces balance. Functions, partial derivatives, logarithmic relationships, and the chain rule also allow interconnected macroeconomic variables to be analyzed systematically. In the final content chapter, we will bring these mathematical tools together and focus on the broader process of translating economic problems into mathematical models, solving calculus-based economic problems, and interpreting their results in economically meaningful terms.

Chapter 8: Applying Calculus to Economic Models

The most valuable use of calculus in economics is not solving an isolated derivative or integral. It is using mathematical tools to investigate an economic problem from beginning to end. A real economic question must first be translated into variables and functional relationships, the appropriate calculus technique must then be selected, and the mathematical result must finally be translated back into economic meaning. This process requires more than computational ability because an equation can be solved correctly while still being interpreted incorrectly. In this chapter, we will bring together the techniques developed throughout the book and focus on constructing economic models, solving calculus-based problems systematically, and determining what the resulting mathematics actually tells us about economic behavior.

Translating Economic Problems Into Mathematical Models

An economic model begins with a question.

A firm might ask how much output it should produce to maximize profit. A consumer might want to determine the affordable combination of goods that maximizes utility. An analyst might want to measure how sensitive demand is to price. A macroeconomic model might examine how capital changes through time as investment and depreciation interact.

Before calculus can answer any of these questions, the economic relationships must be expressed mathematically.

This requires several basic steps:

- Identify the economic objective or question.
- Define the relevant variables and their units.
- Determine which variables are endogenous and which are treated as given.
- Identify the functional relationships connecting the variables.
- Determine whether any constraints limit the feasible choices.
- Select the calculus technique appropriate for the economic question.

Suppose a firm faces the inverse demand function:

$P(q) = 120 - 0.2q$

and has total cost:

$$C(q) = 1{,}000 + 20q + 0.05q^2$$

The economic question is:

What quantity should the firm produce if it wants to maximize profit within this model?

The first step is not differentiation. We first need to construct the appropriate objective function.

Revenue is:

$$R(q) = P(q)q$$

Therefore:

$$R(q) = (120 - 0.2q)q$$

$$R(q) = 120q - 0.2q^2$$

Profit is revenue minus cost:

$$pi(q) = R(q) - C(q)$$

Substitute the functions:

$$pi(q) = 120q - 0.2q^2 - (1{,}000 + 20q + 0.05q^2)$$

Simplify:

$$pi(q) = 100q - 0.25q^2 - 1{,}000$$

Only now do we have the mathematical model needed for optimization.

The choice variable is q, and the objective is:

maximize pi(q)

This distinction between constructing and solving a model is important. If we immediately differentiated the inverse demand function, we would calculate:

$dP/dq = -0.2$

That derivative is mathematically correct, but it does not answer the profit-maximization question.

The mathematics must correspond to the economics.

A different question involving the same demand function could require a completely different calculation.

Suppose instead we ask:

How responsive is quantity demanded to price when the market price is $60?

Now the problem concerns elasticity rather than optimization.

We can solve the inverse demand function for q:

$P = 120 - 0.2q$

$0.2q = 120 - P$

$q = 600 - 5P$

Differentiate:

$dq/dP = -5$

At:

$P = 60$

quantity demanded is:

$q = 600 - 5(60)$

$q = 300$

Price elasticity is:

$Ed = (dq/dP)(P/q)$

Therefore:

$Ed = (-5)(60/300)$

$Ed = -1$

The same underlying demand relationship has now been used to answer an entirely different economic question.

This demonstrates an important principle: the economic question determines the mathematical operation, not the other way around.

Model construction also requires careful attention to assumptions.

Suppose a firm's production function is:

$Q = 20L^{(1/2)}K^{(1/2)}$

If we calculate:

partial Q / partial L

we are examining how output changes as labor changes while capital is held constant.

That "holding capital constant" condition is part of the interpretation of the partial derivative. If capital is also changing with labor, the partial derivative alone does not describe the total change in output.

Likewise, if we construct:

$C(q)$

we are assuming that the relevant costs can be represented as a function of output within the range being studied.

If:

$Qd = f(P,Y)$

we are assuming that quantity demanded is related to price and income according to the particular functional form chosen for the model.

These assumptions are not merely technical details. They define what the resulting mathematics can legitimately tell us.

Economic modeling therefore requires both simplification and discipline. A useful model does not attempt to include every possible real-world influence, but the analyst must understand which relationships have been included and which have been held outside the model.

Solving Calculus-Based Economic Problems

Once an economic problem has been translated into an appropriate mathematical model, the next task is determining how to solve it.

The calculus technique depends on the structure of the question.

A useful way to distinguish among common problems is:

- Use derivatives when the question concerns a rate of change.
- Use partial derivatives when a function contains several independent variables and one relationship must be isolated.
- Use first and second derivatives when investigating maxima, minima, or curvature.

- Use constrained optimization when the decision-maker faces a binding limitation.

- Use integrals when the question concerns accumulation or areas associated with economic curves.

- Use derivatives with respect to time when analyzing dynamic economic relationships.

Consider again the profit function:

pi(q) = 100q - 0.25q^2 - 1,000

Differentiate:

pi'(q) = 100 - 0.5q

Set the first derivative equal to zero:

100 - 0.5q = 0

Therefore:

0.5q = 100

q* = 200

Now check the second derivative:

pi''(q) = -0.5

Because:

pi''(q) < 0

the profit function is concave, confirming that the stationary point represents a maximum.

The corresponding price is:

$P(200) = 120 - 0.2(200)$

$P(200) = 80$

The mathematical solution therefore gives:

$q^* = 200$

$P^* = 80$

But we can also verify the result through marginal analysis.

Revenue was:

$R(q) = 120q - 0.2q^2$

Therefore:

$MR(q) = 120 - 0.4q$

Cost was:

$C(q) = 1{,}000 + 20q + 0.05q^2$

Therefore:

$MC(q) = 20 + 0.1q$

Set marginal revenue equal to marginal cost:

$120 - 0.4q = 20 + 0.1q$

Subtract 20:

$100 - 0.4q = 0.1q$

Therefore:

$100 = 0.5q$

$q^* = 200$

The two methods produce the same result because:

$pi'(q) = MR(q) - MC(q)$

The ability to approach the same economic problem from different mathematical directions can be useful for checking a solution.

Now consider a different type of problem.

Suppose inverse demand is:

$P(q) = 90 - 0.25q$

and the market price is:

$P^* = 30$

We want to calculate consumer surplus.

First determine quantity demanded:

$30 = 90 - 0.25q$

$60 = 0.25q$

$q^* = 240$

Because the question concerns an area between the demand curve and market price, we use integration:

CS = integral from 0 to 240 of [(90 - 0.25q) - 30] dq

Simplify:

CS = integral from 0 to 240 of (60 - 0.25q) dq

Integrate:

CS = [60q - 0.125q^2] from 0 to 240

Evaluate:

CS = 60(240) - 0.125(240^2)

CS = 14,400 - 7,200

CS = $7,200

The structure of the question told us that integration, rather than optimization, was appropriate.

Now consider a multivariable problem.

Suppose production is:

Q = 5L^(0.6)K^(0.4)

and we want to determine how output responds to additional labor while capital remains fixed.

We calculate:

MPL = partial Q / partial L

Therefore:

MPL = 3L^(-0.4)K^(0.4)

If instead we want the marginal product of capital:

MPK = partial Q / partial K

Therefore:

MPK = 2L^(0.6)K^(-0.6)

Again, the economic question determines which derivative we need.

More complicated problems may require several calculus techniques in sequence.

Suppose a model asks us to:

1. Construct a demand function.
2. Derive total revenue.
3. Calculate marginal revenue.
4. Construct total cost.

5. Calculate marginal cost.
6. Determine the profit-maximizing output.
7. Verify the second-order condition.
8. Determine the corresponding market price.

Although the calculations are connected, each answers a different part of the economic problem.

A systematic approach can reduce errors. When solving a calculus-based economic problem, work through the following sequence:

- Write down what the problem is asking.
- Define every variable before calculating.
- Write the relevant economic relationship.
- Construct any missing functions.
- Determine the appropriate calculus operation.
- Perform the calculation.
- Check mathematical conditions and constraints.
- Substitute the solution back into the relevant economic functions.
- Check the units.

- Interpret the result.

Checking units is particularly useful.

Suppose:

$dC/dq = 25$

If C is measured in dollars and q is measured in units of output, then the derivative has units of:

dollars per unit of output

That immediately suggests a marginal cost interpretation.

If:

$dQ/dt = 500$

and Q represents units of output while t is measured in years, the derivative has units of:

units of output per year

If an elasticity calculation produces:

-1.4

the result has no units because elasticity is a proportional measure.

Units can therefore help determine whether a mathematical result has been constructed and interpreted correctly.

Interpreting Mathematical Results in Economic Terms

A calculation is not complete when a number appears at the end of an equation. Economic analysis requires us to explain what that number represents and what conclusions can reasonably be drawn from it.

Suppose we determine:

$MC(100) = 35$

An incomplete interpretation would be:

"Marginal cost is 35."

A better interpretation is:

At an output level of 100 units, total cost is increasing at a rate of approximately $35 per additional unit of output.

The second interpretation identifies the variable, the location at which the derivative is evaluated, and the units of the result.

The same principle applies to elasticity.

Suppose:

$Ed = -1.5$

The important conclusion is not merely that elasticity equals negative 1.5. The magnitude exceeds 1, meaning demand is locally elastic at the point being analyzed. A 1 percent increase in price is associated locally with approximately a 1.5 percent decrease in quantity demanded, under the model and for sufficiently small changes.

Similarly, suppose:

partial Q / partial Y = 0.04

where Q represents quantity demanded and Y represents income measured in thousands of dollars.

The interpretation is not that a one-dollar increase in income raises demand by 0.04 units.

Because Y is measured in thousands of dollars, a one-unit increase in Y represents a $1,000 increase in income. The units built into the model determine the meaning of the derivative.

Optimization results require even more care.

Suppose:

q* = 200

Before declaring this the "optimal output," several questions should be considered:

- Is q = 200 feasible?

- Does it satisfy the relevant first-order condition?

- Does the second-order condition support a maximum?

- Are there boundaries that also need to be evaluated?

- Is the solution economically meaningful?

- What assumptions were used to construct the revenue and cost functions?

A mathematically correct stationary point can still fail to be the relevant economic optimum if it lies outside the feasible range.

Suppose:

$0 <= q <= 150$

but unconstrained optimization gives:

$q^* = 200$

The firm cannot produce 200 units within the stated constraint.

The analyst must then examine the feasible set rather than report the unconstrained result as the final answer.

The same principle applies to consumer optimization.

A mathematical solution might produce:

$X^* = -4$

but negative consumption may not be economically feasible.

The mathematics has produced a result, but the economic restrictions of the problem tell us that the solution cannot represent an admissible consumption bundle.

Economic interpretation also requires distinguishing between mathematical models and predictions about the real world.

Suppose a demand model is:

$Q = 500 - 5P$

The derivative:

$dQ/dP = -5$

is an exact property of that mathematical function.

Whether actual consumer demand changes by exactly five units when price changes by one unit is a separate empirical question. The calculus tells us what follows from the model, while the usefulness of the model depends on how appropriately it represents the economic environment being studied.

This distinction becomes particularly important when working with estimated economic functions.

Suppose statistical analysis produces:

Q = 1,000 - 6P + 0.03Y

Calculus can tell us immediately that:

partial Q / partial P = -6

and:

partial Q / partial Y = 0.03

Those derivatives are mathematical properties of the estimated function. Their broader economic usefulness depends on the quality of the data, estimation method, model specification, and assumptions underlying the analysis.

Calculus provides logical precision within the model. It does not eliminate the need to evaluate the model itself.

Interpretation should therefore answer several questions:

- What economic variable was calculated?
- At what point or under what conditions was it calculated?
- What are the units?
- What does the sign tell us?
- What does the magnitude tell us?

- What assumptions support the result?
- Is the solution feasible?
- Does the result describe a level, rate of change, proportional response, accumulated quantity, or optimum?

Consider:

$dK/dt = -50$

If K represents the capital stock and t represents years, the result means that capital is declining at a rate of 50 units per year at that moment.

Now consider:

$(1/K)(dK/dt) = -0.02$

This tells us that the capital stock is declining at an instantaneous proportional rate of 2 percent per year.

The two expressions describe the same general direction of change, but they provide different information.

Likewise:

$C'(q) > 0$

tells us that total cost is increasing with output.

$C''(q) > 0$

tells us that the rate at which total cost increases is itself increasing.

And:

pi'(q) = 0

tells us that profit is stationary with respect to output at that point, but additional analysis is required before concluding that profit has been maximized.

This ability to distinguish among mathematical statements is central to advanced economic reasoning.

The equations themselves are often only the beginning. The deeper objective is to understand the economic relationships they describe.

Last Thoughts

Applying calculus to economic models requires three connected abilities: translating an economic question into mathematics, selecting and performing the appropriate calculus, and interpreting the resulting mathematics in economic terms. Derivatives, partial derivatives, optimization conditions, and integrals become useful only when they correspond to the structure of the problem being studied. A profit-maximization question requires a different approach from an elasticity calculation, a surplus problem requires different mathematics from a marginal productivity problem, and a dynamic macroeconomic relationship must account for how variables change through time. As economic models become more advanced, the equations may contain more variables, constraints, and interacting relationships, but the analytical process remains recognizable. Begin with the economics, construct the model carefully, use calculus to investigate the relationship, check the mathematical and economic conditions, and interpret the result within the assumptions and units of the model.

Last Thoughts

Economics becomes more powerful when mathematical tools allow us to move beyond describing relationships and begin analyzing precisely how those relationships behave. Throughout this book, calculus has provided a framework for studying rates of change, marginal relationships, optimization, responsiveness, accumulation, and dynamic economic processes. The individual techniques are important, but the larger objective is learning to recognize the mathematical structure underneath an economic question and understand what the resulting calculations mean. A derivative is not simply an operation performed on a function, an integral is not simply an area calculation, and an optimization condition is not simply an equation to solve. Each becomes economically meaningful when connected to the behavior, constraints, incentives, and tradeoffs represented by the model.

Connecting Calculus to Economic Reasoning

Economic reasoning often begins before any equation is written. We first identify the behavior or relationship we want to understand, determine which variables are relevant, and consider how those variables interact. Calculus becomes useful once that economic reasoning has been translated into a mathematical structure.

This distinction is important because knowing how to differentiate a function does not automatically mean knowing which function should be differentiated.

Consider several questions we have encountered throughout the book:

- How does quantity demanded respond to a change in price?
- How does total cost change when a firm increases production?
- What quantity maximizes profit?
- How should a consumer allocate a limited budget between goods?
- How much consumer surplus exists at a particular market outcome?
- How does the capital stock evolve as investment and depreciation change through time?

Each question involves calculus, but each requires a different mathematical approach.

If we want to determine how quantity demanded changes with price, we may calculate:

dQ/dP

If demand depends on several variables and we want to isolate the effect of income, we may calculate:

partial Q / partial Y

If we want to maximize profit, we construct:

pi(q) = R(q) - C(q)

and investigate:

pi'(q) = 0

If we want to measure consumer surplus, we construct a definite integral representing the area between the demand curve and market price.

If we want to study capital accumulation, we may examine a differential relationship such as:

dK/dt = I - delta K

The calculus changes because the economic question changes.

This is one of the most important habits to develop when working with mathematical economics: begin with the economic meaning rather than searching immediately for a formula.

A useful analytical sequence is:

- Identify what the economic problem is asking.
- Determine which quantities are variables and which are parameters or given values.
- Identify the economic relationship connecting those quantities.
- Determine whether the question concerns a level, rate of change, optimum, proportional response, accumulated quantity, or dynamic process.
- Select the mathematical method appropriate for that relationship.
- Solve the mathematics.
- Return to the economic question and interpret the result.

This final step deserves particular attention.

Suppose:

$C'(200) = 40$

The calculation becomes economically useful when we understand that, if C represents dollars of total cost and q represents units of output, total cost is increasing at approximately \$40 per additional unit around an output of 200 units.

Likewise:

$Ed = -2$

becomes economically meaningful when we recognize that quantity demanded is locally proportionally more responsive than price and demand is elastic at the point being analyzed.

A result such as:

$pi'(q^*) = 0$

does not automatically mean that q* maximizes profit. We still need to examine the second-order condition, feasibility, boundaries, and other relevant features of the model.

Economic reasoning therefore continues after the calculus has been completed.

The mathematics tells us what follows from the model. Economic reasoning tells us how to understand that result.

Strengthening Mathematical Economic Intuition

Mathematical intuition develops when equations begin to communicate economic information before every calculation has been completed.

Consider:

$dQd/dP < 0$

Even without numerical values, we can recognize that quantity demanded decreases locally as price increases.

If:

$dQs/dP > 0$

quantity supplied increases locally with price.

If:

$C''(q) > 0$

the slope of the cost function is increasing, meaning marginal cost rises as output increases.

If:

$U''(x) < 0$

for a one-variable utility representation, utility is concave over the relevant region, which can be associated with diminishing marginal utility.

If:

$pi'(q) > 0$

profit is increasing locally as output increases.

If:

$pi'(q) < 0$

profit is decreasing locally as output increases.

These mathematical expressions contain economic information.

The same intuition can be developed for optimization.

Suppose:

MR > MC

The firm gains more additional revenue than additional cost from a small increase in output, so profit can rise locally by increasing production.

If:

MR < MC

additional output contributes more to cost than revenue, so further production lowers profit locally.

The condition:

MR = MC

then becomes easier to understand because it represents the point where the marginal forces influencing profit balance at an interior stationary solution.

Consumer optimization follows a similar logic.

Suppose:

MUx/Px > MUy/Py

The consumer receives more marginal utility per unit of expenditure from X than from Y. Under the assumptions of an interior consumer-choice model, reallocating some spending toward X can improve utility.

At the optimum:

MUx/Px = MUy/Py

The consumer has no marginal gain from reallocating a small amount of expenditure between the goods.

Integration can also become intuitive.

When we write:

integral from 0 to q* of P(q)dq

we should eventually recognize this as an accumulation of price values across quantities. Depending on whether P(q) represents demand, supply, or another economic relationship, that area can acquire a specific economic interpretation.

Similarly:

integral from a to b of MC(q)dq

represents the accumulated change in total cost as output moves from a to b.

Developing this intuition requires looking beyond the mathematical symbol and asking what each component represents.

The sign of a derivative matters.

The magnitude matters.

The units matter.

The point at which the derivative is evaluated matters.

The variables held constant matter.

The curvature of the function matters.

The feasible set matters.

Together, these details determine what an equation tells us economically.

Graphical reasoning can reinforce this intuition even when a graph is not physically drawn. If a derivative is positive, imagine a curve rising as we move from left to right. If a derivative becomes zero and then negative, imagine the function reaching a peak and beginning to fall. If the second derivative is positive, imagine the slope becoming increasingly positive or less negative as the variable increases.

The objective is not to replace calculation with intuition. Instead, intuition gives us a way to evaluate whether our calculations make sense.

If a downward-sloping demand function produces a positive own-price derivative when we expected a negative one, we should check the algebra and the function.

If a profit-maximization problem produces a negative quantity, we should investigate whether the stationary point lies outside the economically feasible set.

If an elasticity result has monetary units attached to it, something is wrong because elasticity is unit-free.

If an integral intended to represent consumer surplus produces a negative value under ordinary conditions, we should check whether the curves or limits were entered in the correct order.

These checks make mathematical intuition an important form of error detection.

As the models become more advanced, this intuition becomes even more valuable because longer calculations create more opportunities for small algebraic or conceptual errors.

Moving Into More Advanced Economic Analysis

The calculus used throughout this book provides a foundation rather than an endpoint. More advanced economics expands many of the same ideas into models involving several variables, multiple constraints, dynamic systems, uncertainty, strategic behavior, and statistical estimation.

The mathematical tools encountered here naturally lead into several areas of further study:

- **Multivariable calculus**, for economic models containing several interacting variables.
- **Constrained optimization**, for decisions involving multiple limitations and choice variables.
- **Matrix algebra**, for systems containing many equations and variables.
- **Differential equations**, for models describing economic adjustment through continuous time.
- **Difference equations**, for models describing economic adjustment across discrete periods.
- **Probability and statistics**, for analyzing uncertainty and economic data.
- **Econometrics**, for estimating economic relationships and evaluating empirical evidence.

- **Dynamic optimization**, for decisions in which current choices influence future opportunities and outcomes.

The economic concepts also become more sophisticated.

Consumer theory can progress from relatively simple utility functions to expenditure minimization, indirect utility, compensated demand, and comparative statics.

Producer theory can move into cost minimization, conditional factor demand, returns to scale, and more complicated technologies.

Market analysis can incorporate strategic interactions, imperfect competition, taxes, externalities, and welfare effects.

Macroeconomic analysis can develop into dynamic models of consumption, savings, investment, capital accumulation, productivity, and growth.

Although these topics introduce additional mathematics, many rely on ideas already developed here.

Consider a general optimization problem:

maximize $f(x)$

subject to:

$g(x) = c$

The notation can become more complicated when x represents a vector containing several choice variables, but the underlying economic problem remains familiar: choose among feasible alternatives to obtain the greatest attainable value of an objective.

Likewise, a dynamic model may contain:

$dx/dt = F(x)$

The function F may become considerably more complicated, but the central question remains recognizable: how does x change through time?

A multivariable economic model might contain:

$Y = F(X1, X2, X3, ...)$

The number of variables may increase, but partial derivatives still help isolate how Y responds to changes in individual variables while others are held constant.

This is why a strong understanding of the fundamentals matters more than memorizing a large collection of formulas.

When encountering a new model, ask:

- What is being explained?
- What is being chosen?

- What is being held constant?
- What is changing?
- What is being maximized or minimized?
- What constraints apply?
- What does the derivative represent?
- What does the solution mean economically?

Those questions provide continuity as the mathematics becomes more advanced.

Calculus also makes it possible to see connections among economic topics that may initially appear unrelated. Consumer optimization and profit maximization both involve objective functions. Marginal utility and marginal product both arise from derivatives. Consumer surplus and producer surplus both involve definite integrals. Economic growth and capital accumulation both involve variables changing through time.

The specific economic interpretation changes, but the mathematical structures repeat.

Recognizing those structures is one of the major advantages of studying economics through calculus.

Last Thoughts

Learning calculus in an economic context is ultimately about learning to think simultaneously in mathematical and economic terms. A function represents a relationship, a derivative measures how that relationship changes, a second derivative provides information about how the rate of change evolves, an optimization condition identifies economically important choices, and an integral allows marginal quantities or areas to be accumulated across an interval. The mathematics becomes most useful when every symbol remains connected to a variable, every calculation remains connected to a question, and every result is interpreted within the assumptions of the model. From here, more advanced economic analysis can introduce additional variables, constraints, dynamic relationships, and mathematical techniques, but the foundation remains the same: define the economic problem carefully, represent it mathematically, analyze it systematically, and understand what the solution actually says about the economic relationship being studied.

About the Author

Roggie "Raj" Clark is an entrepreneur and a 10-year marketing professional with a proven track record in e-commerce and digital business growth. Having built and managed successful online stores with thousands of sales and consulted for numerous marketing clients, Roggie has mastered the intricacies of online marketing, branding, and consumer behavior. He has also written several popular books on digital marketing, SEO (search engine optimization), and programming (HTML, CSS, and JavaScript).

As a former marketing manager at a fintech company—a role he secured through his own marketing and financial expertise—Roggie gained firsthand experience in financial strategy and wealth-building. This journey inspired him to share insights with amateur investors, helping them save money, make smarter financial decisions, and build long-term wealth. Raj currently lives in Maryland with his sister and niece.

www.ingramcontent.com/pod-product-compliance
Lightning Source LLC
LaVergne TN
LVHW050812061126
851857LV00012B/773